DIY VPN

Control Your Own VPN

by J Harvey

July 2019

DIY VPN: Control Your Own VPN

Copyright ©2019 by J Harvey

ISBN: 978-1079165135

Disclaimer

Trademarks

Inquiries

Please refer all inquiries to vpn@diy-vpn.com.

Cover photo: "Tunnel Long Exposure, Shanghai" by Manuel Joseph.

Contents

Contents

Preface

Using a VPN to protect your online privacy is a very hot topic, but most of the discussion too often revolves around which VPN service to use... only rarely does anyone mention how quick, easy, and inexpensive it is to set up and maintain control of your own secure VPN server.

While it may *sound* intimidating, the reality is that installing and using your own VPN server defies the old tech adage that you can't have a good, fast, *and* cheap solution. It's good, fast, cheap *and* a great learning experience... and actually a lot of fun!

By the time you're a few chapters into this guide, you'll be able to launch and connect to a personal VPN server in less than ten minutes... pretty much whenever and wherever you want.

We'll also help remove any speedbumps you might hit and will give you the tools and knowledge you need to get up and running quickly, even if you're completely new to network security, Linux operating systems, and server software.

We'll go beyond the basics to discuss important aspects of your deployment, like:

- How do you verify you've got it right?

- How do you transfer VPN connection information to your phone quickly, easily, and *securely*?

- Can you use your VPN server to block ads? (Yes, and it's amazing!)

- How do you secure and monitor your system after you've got it up and running?

- What can we do to make our system stronger and more secure?

And what about setting up VPN connections that have incomplete support, like ChromeOS on the Chromebook? In researching this guide, I found forum posts from people who spent days (and even months!) trying to get things working for computers that had limited native OpenVPN support...and eventually gave up.

It doesn't have to be that way, and it *shouldn't* be that way. The purpose of this book is to ensure that *you* don't give up.

Who should read this?

You should! Especially if you're:

- Interested in taking control of your digital privacy.

- Looking to kickstart a VPN deployment in five minutes.

- Seeking a nuts-to-bolts primer on OpenVPN installation and configuration on a cloud-based server.

If you want to learn a few networking and system administration skills with a fun project that you can put to immediate use, you should find something useful here.

In this guide, we'll first demonstrate speed and simplicity by setting up and connecting to a VPN server quickly using an automated script on Amazon Lightsail, a light front-end interface to Amazon EC2.

We'll then move on to even more hands-on installation and configuration using Amazon EC2.

Along the way, you'll gain experience and familiarity with OpenVPN and web server software, networking concepts, basic network and command line tools in Linux, intrusion detection software, and more.

The greatest thing about cloud services is that you can explore and experiment without fear: You can set up your own on-demand VPN server in under five minutes, try it out for a bit, and if you're not in love with it, tear it down. At the end of the day, you've only spent a few pennies for data (not even that, if you're new to AWS and using Amazon's free tier) and you've gained a lot of useful knowledge and experience.

And, by the time you finish this guide, you may find a new passion for network server software and security... because it really is a lot of fun!

Prerequisites

You don't need much to get started, just an Internet connection and:

A computer! Alright, you may actually be resourceful and clever enough to do everything in this guide on your mobile device (and technically, you could run *Launching a VPN and Web Server in Under Five Minutes* using *just* your smartphone), but it'll be a lot easier on a laptop or desktop computer.

 If you purchased this guide as an ebook from Amazon, you can access it at https://read.amazon.com on your desktop. This makes it easy to cut and paste commands as needed throughout the book.

In this guide, we assume you're using Microsoft Windows, macOS, or any Linux distribution, like Ubuntu. All software will be installed on remote systems, so you'll pretty much just be using your computer to connect to them.

An Amazon Web Services Account. If you don't have an account, fire up a browser and navigate to https://aws.amazon.com and click **Create A Free Account**.

If you're already an Amazon user, this is super-quick: simply log in using the credentials you use to log into Amazon.com.

Be aware that while the actual use of a server instance is free for free tier users for the first year (up to 750 hours per month), and data transfer *in* is free, data transfer *out* of EC2 after your first free GB is $.09 cents USD per GB (in the US-East region; prices may vary slightly across regions).

So, for example, if you downloaded 10GB of data through EC2, you'd be charged 81 cents USD.

Amazon Lightsail is free for one month, and $3.50 per month for the smallest server size (which is what we'll need for our personal VPN server) each month thereafter.

For more information about Amazon's pricing, see https://aws.amazon.com/pricing. For information about their free tier program, see https://aws.amazon.com/free/.

An SSH (Secure SHell) client. If you're a Windows user without the Windows Subsystem for Linux (which provides an ssh client), you can use PuTTY. We'll walk through downloading and configuring it later on. If you're a Linux or MacOS user, you can run ssh directly from your terminal or console.

While it's helpful to be comfortable using a text editor on the command line, it's not a prerequisite. The Amazon Linux AMI we'll use comes stock with the vi text editor (my personal favorite) and nano — if you're new to Linux and the command line, nano's a fantastic choice because the instructions right are at the bottom of the window. If neither of those strike your fancy, you can always install your favorite editor on-demand.

If you're not comfortable on the command line, don't worry! You'll get there and there's nothing to be afraid of — we'll be working on something that you can build and break at will while you're learning.

A web browser. We assume you're using Mozilla Firefox, Google Chrome, or Apple Safari.

Optionally, a mobile phone. This is truly the reason this guide exists — setting up proxies for cell phones is nearly impossible for a layperson, but a VPN connection *just works* (and is an quick and easy way to block ads and ad-delivered malware). This guide walks you through connecting Android and iPhone devices to your VPN server as well as Linux, Windows, macOS, and Chromebook systems.

This guide is targeted towards novices just starting out with AWS and server software configuration and should be usable even by people unfamiliar with the command line or Linux operating system. You shouldn't — and don't — have to be an expert to set this kind of software up or lock it down for personal use.

Formatting Conventions

Code and shell commands are displayed using fixed-width font.

Commands that are considered part of the same line but are too long to fit in a single column are separated by backslashes (\). For example, the following command:

```
git clone https://a-very-long-url-that-won-t-fit-on-one-line /tmp/\
a-very-long-url
```

would be entered at the command line as a single line:

```
git clone https://a-very-long-url-that-won-t-fit-on-one-line /tmp/a-very-long-url
```

Shell commands that you type on the server and not locally typically begin with the following shell prompt as an indicator `[ec2-user~]$` — i.e., you type everything after the $). In rare cases, with very long commands that are important to fit into one line, we've removed the shell prompt; but the `sudo` that appears at the beginning and instructions will make it obvious where to enter the command!

The terms "instance," "server," "host," and "system" are used interchangeably throughout this guide, depending on context — but they all refer to the same entity: the cloud-based system on which you install and configure software.

1

Introduction

Before we dive head-first into our VPN server project, let's start at the very beginning. We should first understand what it is we're going to be building. It's especially important to understand in which ways a personal VPN protects our privacy, and in which ways it does not.

1.1   What's a VPN?

VPN stands for *Virtual Private Network*. We have *private* networks and *public* networks. Your home network is a good example of a private network. Each computer or mobile device is physically connected to your router via an Ethernet cable or using wireless networking (wifi), and you can then communicate with other devices on your private network. These are *physical private networks*.

For example, say you send a file to your printer, which also resides on your private network. All communication between you and your printer stays inside your private network and should not be seen by the outside world. Each of the devices on the private side of your router — that is, inside your *network perimeter* — are given reserved IP (Internet Protocol) addresses that are never used on the open Internet (addresses like 172.16.x.x or 10.x.x.x) and they use these addresses to contact each other.

When you connect to a resource on the Internet, which is a *public* network, your network traffic is funneled through your router, and the public IP address associated with your router — not the address you have on your computer — is what the web sites you visit see.

When you add a VPN to the mix, your computer connects to and establishes an encrypted connection with your VPN server whenever you attempt to connect to the Internet. We refer to this encrypted connection as a *secure tunnel* — and your Internet traffic is then routed through this "tunnel" directly to the VPN server, which then passes it on to the greater Internet. Because the data is encrypted and bundled up on its way to the VPN server, your router and ISP pass it on through, without being able to inspect it.

They *can* see that the data stream exists, but they cannot perform deep inspection of the traffic itself as it is encrypted and encapsulated. In addition, because traffic is sent from the VPN to its ultimate destination, servers on the Internet see your VPN's IP address and *not* your home router's address or your mobile device's address.

In basic terms, a VPN acts as an extension of your home network; it acts as a router *outside* your home router and extends your private network *virtually*.

1.2 Why Use a VPN?

There are a number of practical reasons you might want to use a VPN.

Keep your location and Internet Service Provider private. Limited sensitive information, like your approximate location and Internet Service provider, can be gleaned purely from your router's IP address.

Ever hear the story about Internet sleuths discovering that Congress members and oil companies were editing their own Wikipedia entries?[1] Wikipedia publicly logs the IP address of anyone who edits a page and IP ranges owned by corporations and government agencies are publicly known, so Wikipedia edits can then be correlated with their editors, or at the very least correlated with the entity for whom the editor works! (Let's hope that they don't read this guide, government and corporate PR *should* be transparent!)

Avoid interception while using public wifi connections. Because your traffic is transmitted through a direct and encrypted connection to your VPN server, eavesdroppers that share the same private network (think: coffee shop, hotel, or airport connection) cannot decrypt any traffic that would normally be sent unencrypted, as it's all bundled up and transmitted through the encrypted channel.

Avoid privacy invasion and ad injection. When using a VPN, your ISP, mobile carrier, or local wifi provider cannot intercept your network traffic to pick out points of data to save and sell to marketers. I noticed that shortly after I started watching Spanish language TV shows and films in Netflix, web sites I visited started to offer me the ability to switch my language to Spanish and other streaming services began serving me local cable commercials... in Spanish. Is it possible that not all of my TV streaming traffic was encrypted?[2] How did they get this info? As a consumer with no insight into these companies' business practices, it's hard for us to know for sure. But as paying customers, it's not our responsibility to make it easier for them.

Not only does a VPN's encryption and encapsulation capabilities keep our private data from the prying eyes of our Internet providers, it also prevents them from injecting their own code into our web pages, as Comcast[3] and other Internet service providers have done in the past and continue to do.

Connect to "local" network resources when physically remote. VPNs can be configured to connect you to network resources in other private networks. In fact, this was their original purpose. You may have used this configuration to access your office remotely: while you might be physically separate from your office, when you connect to your corporate VPN, it affords you access to network resources inside your company and you are connected virtually. In this guide, however, we'll be configuring the VPN as what is called a tunnel connection (we pass right through and do not access additional resources inside the VPN's network), not a *tap* connection (where other devices connected to the VPN can communicate with each other — this is often referred to as *bridging*).

Workaround blocks on public wifi networks. You may find yourself on a network that blocks your access to certain resources. Here's an example I recently ran into...while visiting a brewery with an exceptionally comfortable and work-friendly outside patio, I needed to access a system to get a quick bit of work done. Now, I'd configured the system to only allow me in if I'm coming from my VPN, but that was no problem, takes just a second to connect to the VPN...however...the brewery's wily systems administrator blocked UDP traffic, and I couldn't connect to my everyday VPN! No worries, I could log into a different open system using ssh and pop over that way. Nope! Foiled again — that wily systems admin blocked port 22! A formidable opponent! Thank goodness I had a quick way to launch a VPN on any random port or protocol...I quickly launched a new VPN server on TCP port 2222 — et voila, back to work in five minutes.

Speed up your connection (believe it or not!). You might worry about speed here — does adding the extra "hop" between you and your destination slow down your connection? It's possible, but because the VPN firstly acts as a pipe or tunnel, passing your traffic along the wire without stopping to inspect it, the bump in the road is minimal, especially if you're hosting your VPN with a service provider with prodigious resources. In fact, because your traffic is encapsulated and encrypted, your ISP or mobile network carrier can no longer easily deprioritize certain types of traffic, like media streaming. This is often referred to as *traffic shaping*. Using a VPN may actually increase your speed in many cases because your traffic is not as easily profiled and thus is less likely to be throttled or blocked.

Avoid DNS Leaks. When your ISP assigns your router or computer with an IP address, it also sends a list of Domain Name Service providers, or *DNS servers.* DNS servers hold a master database, a sort of "phone book" that keeps track of which domain name belongs to which IP address. When you visit https://www.duckduckgo.com in your web browser, for example, your computer first contacts a DNS server to perform a lookup that tells it which IP address to use to get there.

Even if an entity has no view into your web traffic itself because you're using https (HTTP over TLS, which is encrypted), the sites you visit and DNS lookups can still deliver a lot of private information. For example, if you look up some things on webmd.com a few times a day, then access diabetes.com several times, someone (or more accurately, some program or application) seeing these queries could intuit that a household member may have diabetes... and you know, maybe that explains all of those drug ads you've been deluged with lately (it could be the cookies in your browser, too — but that's another book!).

This is also why it's important, even if you're using a VPN, to ensure that the VPN is properly configured to route you to DNS servers you trust not to store and share your lookups.

Avoid DNS Hijacking. We just mentioned the DNS servers your ISP or mobile network provider use to help you quickly access web sites. In some cases, your ISP sends your computer a list of its own DNS servers that are configured to redirect specific domain names.

Often this is ostensibly to speed up your browsing experience: pages take less time to load if they're hosted on the cable company's site and not remotely — however, these sites can be "stale" or out-of-date, and what's worse: they can be used to surreptitiously intercept your activity.

One common case is where you visit Google, but instead of going directly to Google, your ISP's DNS servers may send you to *their* cached (saved) copy of Google's site. When you enter your terms into this cached Google site, your ISP then forwards the query to Google — and you're none the wiser about the interception: but now your ISP knows what you were searching for. This is called *DNS hijacking.*

It's pretty slick: unless you happened to look at your network connections when you accessed the web site, you'd never know it was happening.

Block ads. You can configure your VPN server as a DNS server for connected clients and can block ads for any device that uses the VPN. This is a beautiful feature on mobile devices — no need to install ad-blocking software, just connect to your VPN and browse away! Ad blocking also saves you from those fly-by-night ad network hijackers that pop up scammy redirect links when all you're trying to do is read the news.

Secure your network configuration on mobile devices. It's easy to manually configure DNS servers on your laptop or desktop computer, but have you ever tried it on a mobile phone, especially an iPhone? Virtually impossible. When using a properly-configured VPN, all you have to do is turn it on, and if your VPN is properly configured, you're properly routed.

While a (properly-configured) VPN will help keep you safe from the threats we've just described — network traffic-based data gathering, ISP ad injection, DNS hijacking, traffic shaping, malware surreptitiously distributed by compromised ad networks, and exploitation by nosy neighbors at the coffee shop — it is not a panacea.

1.3   Does a VPN Protect You Completely?

No. A VPN encrypts and protects your network traffic between you and your VPN server, period. This keeps you safe from *some* security and privacy threats on the Internet. Their usage is *part* of a self-protection toolset, not the complete toolset.

While your traffic is encrypted on its path *to* the VPN server, if you're not using a secure web connection (https, for example, instead of http), your traffic will be seen as it exits the VPN, the same way it would be seen as it exits your router when you're not connected to a VPN. You're basically just moving your exposure further away from your home.

And obscuring your home IP address isn't enough to make you completely anonymous: you can be identified using tracking cookies and browser characteristics (often referred to as *browser fingerprinting*). It's probable that you can be uniquely identified by interested parties using just the information the browser provides to web sites in order to function effectively: the fonts on your system combined with your browser plugins and version, and your device's display characteristics.

If you're running a small-scale server for just yourself, a few friends, and/or family, you won't get quite the needle-in-a-haystack IP anonymity you'd get when using a service with tens of thousands of people attached (but conversely, if another user on a public VPN you use is being investigated for illegal activity, there's a chance that your innocuous network activity can be swept up into the dragnet).

Contrary to what some fly-by-night VPN "providers" claim, a VPN will not prevent you from getting computer viruses and malware, they will not anonymize you, and they will not keep you safe from all threats on the Internet. Stay far away from any VPN provider that isn't honest with you about this. Or, even better, keep reading and do it all yourself!

1.4 Why not just use a VPN service?

You may have picked up on something else during our discussion of the network traffic flow between you, the VPN server, and your destination: because the VPN server routes you, the VPN server sees where you're going. Using a third party provider whose configuration may not be secure and whose data policies are opaque can be risky, and in some cases could be even riskier than not using a VPN at all — yet another good reason for *you* to maintain control of the VPN server itself.

When you run your own VPN, you can precisely control who has access to it and what it logs. You can start it up and shut it down, re-configure it at will, granularly control the security level, and understand what's going on under the hood. If you want to use a higher level of encryption or update to a newer version of software, you can do so immediately — no waiting around for your provider to do it.

That said, you may ultimately decide to use a VPN service — but it's worth spending a little time to determine whether you'd rather empower yourself to control your own system, especially in an environment where there are so many unknowns.

Recently, researchers at CSIRO in Australia published a study[4] examining 283 VPN-enabled apps on Android. Of these apps, 67% contained third-party tracking libraries, 84% leaked IPv6 traffic, 66% leaked DNS traffic, 38% contained malware, and *18% didn't even use encrypted tunnels!* Conversely, they found that the user reviews were largely positive — even for the apps that contained malware, didn't encrypt traffic, and leaked data.

There are definitely some great VPN providers out there who care about the privacy and safety of their customers, but it pays to be educated about VPN functionality itself and to know how to verify that your VPN provider is providing the services you expect — and that's one of the skills you'll learn here as you install, configure, and verify your own OpenVPN setup.

Verify, then trust, then verify again!

And with that, we're ready to get started. In the next chapters, we'll walk through the creation and configuration of a basic, secure, and personal VPN server running on Amazon Web Services (AWS). By the time you've finished the guide, you'll be able to:

- Launch and connect to a Linux-based server on both Amazon Lightsail and Amazon EC2.

- Install and configure a secure instance of OpenVPN server.

- Install and configure a secure and password-protected web site running Apache HTTP Web Server where you can download VPN connection files.

- Connect Linux, Microsoft Windows, Apple OSX, Google ChromeBook, iPhone/iPad, and Android devices to your custom VPN server.

- Use basic network tools and other crafty methods to verify that your VPN connection is secure and that your traffic is successfully traversing your VPN server. You can use some of these methods to verify third party VPN server connections, too.

- Install and configure OSSEC, an open source network intrusion detection and log monitoring software package that can help secure your installation.

- Optionally, register a domain name to use with your system, associate it with your server using Amazon's Route 53, and secure it with an auto-renewable SSL certificate from LetsEncrypt.

Using these instructions, you can easily deploy an automated, secure and working VPN and web server in less than ten minutes, and a personally-configured secure, private VPN and web server that only you can access in less than an hour. Add 15 more minutes and you'll have system monitoring and intrusion detection enabled.

So let's get to it!

2

Launching a VPN and Web Server in Five Minutes

Before we tunnel into the depths of VPN configuration, it's useful to demonstrate how quickly you can set up a secure and ready-to-use VPN server with a hands-on exercise using automated scripts.

We'll start by launching and connecting to an OpenVPN-based VPN and secure web server in less than five minutes using Amazon Lightsail and some customized scripts we've cooked up.

Amazon Lightsail is a lighter version of Amazon Web Services' (AWS) Elastic Compute Cloud (EC2) and a nice playground to get started in. You can quickly launch a server and you don't need any software, other than a web browser, to access and manage it. Like AWS EC2, it comes with a free tier. While it doesn't provide free services for an entire year like EC2, for the first month, up to 750 hours is free. After the initiation period, servers start at $3.50/month for up to a terabyte of data transfer.

The $3.50 server is well-suited for a personal VPN and, given the data transfer pricing, likely more economical in the long-run than EC2 for heavy data usage. This is what I personally use to host my own primary VPN server(s).

After we finish, we'll move on to Amazon EC2 itself, which provides a lot more flexibility, and we'll walk through configuration and setup in much more detail so that you have the ability to customize the default settings we use in our automated scripts.

What we are doing here is basically an automated version of what we'll be doing as we progress through the guide.

The installation script will install, configure, and start OpenVPN as the server boots up. It will then install, configure, and start a web server that we'll use to securely transmit our VPN configuration files.

Finally, the script will build those configuration files and deliver them to a password and TLS-protected directory that we can use to download our files and install them — and connect to our VPN!

 The procedures here can cost money. The first month of use for a single server up to 750 hours is free. Each month thereafter is $3.50 per running server (commonly referred to as a *server instance*).

Turn on your stopwatch and let's bootstrap a VPN server!

1. Open Amazon Lightsail (https://lightsail.aws.amazon.com) in a browser. If you've already set up an Amazon Web Services Account, you'll use that same username and password for Lightsail.

2. Click **Create Instance**.

3. Select **Linux/Unix, OS Only**, and then select **Amazon Linux**.

4. In another browser tab, navigate to the following URL to access the DIY VPN launch script:

   https://diy-vpn.com/launch

5. Copy all of the text you see there (on your keyboard, hit CTRL-A to select, then CTRL-C to copy, from #!/bin/bash all the way down to fi).

   What is this? Don't worry if this looks like nonsense to you right now — we'll use the commands in launchscript.sh as our "launch script," which our server instance will execute unattended after it starts up. It will check the operating system version on the Lightsail server, install git — a version control system which holds our installation scripts — and then it will clone our scripts into a directory on the system. It will then run the installer script (build-vpn.sh). By the time we're physically able to log into the system, the script should be busy doing all of our work for us!

6. Go back to the Lightsail tab and click the + **Add Launch Script** link. Paste (CTRL-V) the full script you copied in Step 4 into the box.

7. Choose the **$3.50/First Month Free!** plan.

8. Enter a name for your instance in the **Identify your instance** field (for example, "DIY-VPN") and click **Create Instance.**

   You'll see the instance's status show as *Pending* for twenty seconds or so while your instance loads up. *Pending* should then change to *Running.*

9. Tap the ellipsis menu associated with the instance and select **Manage.**

10. Tap the **Networking** link and scroll down to **Firewall.**

    You'll notice that two rules exist, one for port 22 (so that you can connect to the instance using secure shell, or ssh) and port 80 (the default server web port).

11. Add two new rules by tapping the + **Add Another** link for each rule:

    - Custom **TCP** rule for port 443 (this is for our secure VPN client configuration file web server)

    - Custom **UDP** rule for port 1194 (default port for our VPN server)

12. Click **Save**.

> *i* These ports are open to the world, which is one of a few reasons our setup scripts harden the installation. When you move to later chapters using traditional EC2, you'll see that you can restrict outside access so that only you can access the system.

13. Scroll back up and tap the **Connect** link, then click the **Connect Using SSH** button to open a console connection to your system.

14. Make a note of the **Public IP** address that appears on the left bottom of the console window.

15. Verify that the installation is complete by checking the log file that the script generates as it runs. We'll use a command called `tail` that displays the last lines of a file and add the option `-f` which will display the file in real-time, as it is appended. The last lines of the file will differ based on when the script is run (the numbers represent the date and time, in seconds, that the script was run), if you type `tail -f /tmp/.build-vpn` and then press the *Tab* button, the system will complete it for you.

    ```
    [ec2-user~]$ tail -f /tmp/.build-vpn.log.1562376715
    ```

    You should see an "ALL DONE!" message with instructions on how to proceed.

16. Press CTRL-C to exit your `tail` command, and now let's follow the instructions in the ALL DONE message to locate our configuration file download password.

    The script generates a random password and places it in ec2-user's home directory (`/home/ec2-user`) in a file named `.web` (ec2-user is the default user name for all Amazon EC2 instances).

17. So now, run:

    ```
    cat .web
    ```

    to display the password.

18. Copy the password by selecting the password, right-clicking, and selecting Copy (CTRL-C or CTRL-Shift-C do not work on the Amazon Console).

19. Navigate to `https://your_server_ip/downloads`, where `your_server_ip` is the IP address you noted from the console in step 14 (you can also right-click to copy the full link from the "ALL DONE!" message). You'll see a browser warning us to stop. This is because we're using a self-signed SSL certificate. We'll talk about these in more detail later on — but because we know this is a server under our control, proceed anyway by choosing **Advanced > Proceed** on Google Chrome or **Advanced > Accept the Risk and Continue** on Firefox.

20. When prompted, enter the username `vpn` and the password you copied from the `.web` file.

    You should see a list of files: An ONC and p12 file for use with Google ChromeOS (Chromebook) and an OVPN file for all other platforms.

21. Download the ovpn file if you're connecting using any device other than ChromeOS for ChromeBook. ChromeOS users should download the ONC and p12 files. You can then use it to connect and verify your connection using the following instructions:

    - *Windows* on page 75

    - *macOS* on page 77

    - *Linux* on on page 79

    - *iPhone* on page 81

    - *Android* on page 82

    - *ChromeOS* on page 83

After you're in and connected, you're ready for more advanced topics and it's time to try this out on EC2. Proceed to Launching Your Amazon EC2 Instance on page 17 to continue.

3

Launching Your EC2 Instance

While most of the instructions in this guide can be used with any other service provider, this guide uses Amazon Web Services' Elastic Compute Cloud (EC2) for a number of practical reasons, including:

Amazon's robust ecosystem: We can launch a server, install software, purchase a domain name, configure domain name resolution, and so on, without ever leaving Amazon, which makes it easier to complete all of the tasks we might want to complete in this guide. Here, we're doing everything hands-on from the Amazon Management Console web interface, but we could potentially automate everything — which is pretty powerful. We can also perform every procedure in this guide using a single provider. While the instructions and configurations provided in this guide could be run from pretty much anywhere, by getting comfortable inside a single ecosystem, you'll gain the confidence to deploy these kinds of systems anywhere.

It's inexpensive for small-scale use: If you're new to AWS, you get access to their "free tier" program, which allows you to use micro-instances and other resources for free for up to twelve months. You can still incur charges otherwise, though — while data transfer into AWS is free, outgoing data is not free (as of writing, between 0 and 9 cents per Gigabyte transfer out, depending on how and where it's transferred; see Amazon's pricing documentation for more information). In addition, you can incur charges for unused static IPs and other services if you don't release them. But because you can pause systems, stop them, and release resources, you can keep costs very low.

Extensible: You can preconfigure a system, and then later spin it up on demand. No need to fear "breaking things." If you make a mistake, blow the whole system away and start over.

Geographically diverse: Amazon provides a variety of options for system location — you can host in the US, Europe, South America, and Southeast Asia. If you know you're going to be traveling to Europe, for example, you can set up a server in Frankfurt and enjoy speedy, private downloads when you get there.

You can encrypt your data at rest: The truly paranoid person may never, and should never, trust any service provider completely. It's up to you who you decide to trust with your data and there's always a risk vs. value proposition. Amazon may win for our current use case of spinning up a VPN server to keep our ISP and mobile data carrier from profiling us and protecting us while travelling; it may not ultimately work for all use cases. It's also always worth reviewing a company's data privacy policy before jumping in: Amazon Data Privacy FAQ.

You can, however, apply the instructions here to servers run from any service provider — while the machine image we're using for our server component runs CentOS, the open and community-based version of RedHat Linux, most of the instructions can easily be ported to other Linux-based operating systems. Swap out yum (the software installer for Red Hat-based operating systems like CentOS) for apt (the software installer for Debian-based OSes like Ubuntu), and so on, and you're good to go.

The procedures here can incur costs. If you're a new EC2 user, you automatically get twelve months of "free tier" usage, where you can use 750 hours on a single Linux instance and 750 hours Windows instance per month for free (in this guide, we'll just be using a Linux instance). While "instance hours" - or the actual use of the instance is free for free tier users, and data transfer *in* is free, *data transfer *out* of EC2 after your first free GB is $.09 cents USD per GB,* if you're in the US-East region. So, for example, if you downloaded 10GB of data through EC2, you'd be charged 81 cents USD.For more information about Amazon's free tier program, see https://www.aws.amazon.com/free.

For those who have already used up their free tier pricing (like your author!), the price is currently .10 per hour per instance, and .11 per SSD GB used on EBS in US zones, and a penny more in Europe. Note that these were the prices as of writing, they may change, see https://aws.amazon.com/ec2/pricing for current pricing information.

Amazon does charge per hour used and by the hour. Because of the way they do this, starting and stopping a server (which may run on different hardware each time) three times in an hour may cost a lot more than just allowing your system to run for an hour straight.

Ready to go? The first thing we'll do is log into the AWS Management Console and launch a small server:

1. First, open https://aws.amazon.com, tap **Sign In to the Console** or **AWS My Account > Management Console** and log in.

2. At the upper-right of the page, select the region you'd like to use for your server. Typically, this would be

somewhere close to you to optimize site speed, but in some cases, you may want to store your data in a different country altogether. Amazon has options within the US, Canada, the European Union, the Asia Pacific region, and South America (SÃčo Paolo).

3. From the **Services** menu, select **EC2** from the Compute list. The Resources page appears.

4. Click **Launch Instance.** The Choose AMI page appears.

5. Locate the **Amazon Linux 2 AMI (HVM), SSD Volume Type** image (typically at the top of the Quickstart list; the date and AMI ID will change periodically), ensure that **64-bit (x86)** is selected and click **Select.** The Choose Instance Type page appears.

   About the Amazon Linux AMI: The Amazon Linux 2 AMI is a customized version of CentOS, an open and community-based version of Red Hat Enterprise Linux. Amazon's AMI is lightweight, locked down, contains Amazon-specific tools, and software and security updates are timely. It's also eligible for the free tier if you're a new AWS user.

6. Select **General Purpose – t2.micro** and then click **Next: Configure Instance Details.** The Configure Instance Details page appears.

   Why did we choose the t2.micro instance? The t2.micro server is a small virtual machine with 1 GB of memory backed by EBS. For our purposes — a small, personal server with just a few users, it's a good place to start. Should you find you need more processing power and faster throughput, you can always scale up.

7. We'll keep the defaults on the Instance Details page for our current use case. Click **Next: Add Storage** to continue. The Add Storage page appears.

8. You typically have three options here:

   - Keep the default at 8GB

   - Add additional space

   - Add additional drives.

   Because we're not planning to keep logs on the server and this is a small-scale VPN setup, we'll accept the default (we could even go smaller — a finished setup with a few days of runtime uses less than 2GB).

   After you've gone through the install once, consider your use case for the system. If it's likely you'll be placing large files on the system, you can give yourself more space. If you're eligible for Amazon's free tier, you can add up to 30 GB of storage without incurring charges. You can also choose to add a new volume — this allows you to encrypt the added volume (note that you'll have to mount any volumes you add after the instance boots up and configure them to start up at boot time; they are not automatically mounted).

9. Decide whether you want to keep the snapshot around after you terminate the instance and set **Delete on Termination** accordingly. Amazon *does* charge for hard drive storage (*Elastic Block Storage*, or EBS) even when not actively attached to an instance. It's therefore worth configuring them to be deleted when you *terminate* an instance. Terminating an instance destroys it and deletes all data, whereas *stopping* an instance stops it from running, allowing you to restart it at will later.

   If you don't delete it on termination, you can attach it as a drive to future launched instances.

10. Once you've specified your disk size, click **Next: Add Tags**.

The Add Tags page appears.

11. Click **Add Tag** to add a new tag.

12. In the **Key** field, enter Name and type in a name you'll remember (like DIY-VPN) in the the **Value** field.

    You can also add any additional tags you may need or want to use. Tags can be used to automate and control access for systems and make it easier to search for and organize topologies, billing data, and other types of managed in large deployments. For us, a name should be sufficient. You can add tags later if you need them.

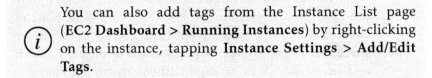 You can also add tags from the Instance List page (**EC2 Dashboard > Running Instances**) by right-clicking on the instance, tapping **Instance Settings > Add/Edit Tags**.

13. Click **Next: Configure Security Group**. The Configure Security Group page appears.

    Security groups control how your system can be accessed. You can create multiple policies and switch them at will, and edit them at any time. The default security policy is configured to keep port 22 (ssh) open to the world. We will absolutely be changing that (keeping port 22 open *to us* so that we can access the server, but disallowing access to anyone else). We'll also open ports to allow us to access our VPN and web servers, while restricting outside connections.

14. First, in the **Name** field, enter **VPN-WEB** and add a description.

15. Next, which IP address are you using to connect to Amazon? If you don't know your external IP, you can visit https://diy-vpn.com/ip or search "What's my IP?" on a search engine like Google or DuckDuckGo and it will helpfully display it.

16. Now that you know your IP, replace 0.0.0.0/0 with y.y.y.y/32 (where y.y.y.y is your IP) in the **Source** field that corresponds with the **TCP 22** rule

> If your IP address changes often, you can open this up a little further — if you know you're always going to be coming from y.y.y.y, for example, you would use 32 as your *subnet mask* (or *netmask*) which specifically restricts access to the single host specified. If you know you bounce around to anywhere within y.y.y.0 to y.y.y.255, then you would use y.y.y.y/24 to 24, which would allow access to any system from those 256 addresses. For most purposes, though, it's a good idea to lock down access to your system only. Start paranoid — you can always make your security policy more permissive later!

17. Click **Add Rule** again, this time using a port of **1194** and protocol of **Custom UDP** (UDP 1194 is the default OpenVPN protocol and port), and enter your IP and netmask.

18. Click **Add Rule** again, and add an entry for **Custom Port TCP** with port **443**. We'll use this port for the secure web server we'll use to host VPN client configuration files.

19. Click **Add Rule** once more, and add an entry for **Custom Port TCP** with port **80**. This is also used for the web server we'll use to host configuration files. While port 80 typically is used by the non-secure (http) listener for the web site, later on, we'll configure our web server to listen on port 80, and pass users over to the secure side (https://*host_name*, running on port 443).

If you are currently connected to the VPN you installed using Amazon Lightsail in the last chapter, you should also add your Amazon Lightsail public IP to the security group for each port.

20. Click **Review Instance Launch**. The Review Instance Launch page appears. If everything looks good, click **Launch**.

21. The Key Pair selector appears. If you have keys already on AWS that you feel appropriate to use here, you can do that. Otherwise, select **Create a new key pair**, give it a name, and click **Download Key Pair**.

22. Save the key pair someplace safe and protect the file — it is the only way you'll be able to log into your system, and if anyone else gets access to it, they could access your system as well (if your security policy permitted network access, that is) — and then click **Launch Instances**.

 While you're waiting for your instance to start up, Amazon provides a friendly note and link to billing alerts. While setting up billing alerts is optional, it's a good idea to set them up. When enabled, Amazon will send you notifications when estimated bills reach a specified threshold. You can use this also to receive a notification if you are using the free usage tier and charges exceed it, or the tier has expired after your twelve-month free period.

Next, we'll use Amazon Elastic IP to set a static IP address for your server, so that you can always reach it at the same address.

3.1 Assigning a Static Public IP Address to Your Instance

For our use case of a quickly-provisioned VPN server, it's not a huge deal to use an ephemeral IP address that may be subject to change on Amazon's whims. However, if you plan to use your VPN for awhile, you should give it a static IP so that it can always be reached the same way.

If you plan to give your VPN server a domain name so that it's easy for others to connect to it, a static IP is a must. A DNS record holds the association between your domain name and IP — if your IP changes, name resolution will fail and your site becomes inaccessible to anyone attempting to reach it by hostname.

When you build another VPN server, you can easily re-assign your static IP to the new instance. Amazon Elastic IPs can be detached and re-associated with your systems, but be aware that Amazon charges half of a penny an hour (at time of publication) for Elastic IPs that are *not* associated to running instances. Therefore, it pays to delete or re-assign them when not in use to avoid incurring any charges. When you terminate an instance, there will be a checkbox you can enable to release the Elastic IP back to Amazon.

To associate a static IP with your instance:

1. In your browser, navigate to the AWS Management Console, log in, and click **EC2**.

2. Under **Network & Security** on the left menu, select **Elastic IPs**. The Elastic IP page appears.

3. Tap **Allocate New Address**. The Allocate New Address page appears.

4. Keep the default the **VPC** (Virtual Private Cloud) and **Amazon Pool** radio buttons selected and click **Allocate**. You'll receive a message that shows that the request succeeded, along with the IP address.

5. Click **Close**. You'll be returned to the Elastic IP page.

6. Select the IP you just generated, click **Actions**, and then select **Associate Address**.

> If no instances appear in the list, you may have accidentally accepted the default "Classic" option when allocating the address. While Classic is the default option, if you created your AWS account in the last few years, you have a VPC account and not Classic. Cancel the operation, go back to the Allocation page, select the IP, click Actions, then select Release Addresses to delete the Classic IP. Then, allocate a new address, this time using the VPC option.

7. Next to **Resource Type**, accept the default **Instance** option and, from the **Instance** list, select your VPN server instance.

8. Select a **Private IP**. In our case, we only have a single IP available as our system was configured with a single network interface. If you had created an instance with multiple network interfaces, this option allows you to associate an Elastic IP to a specific interface.

9. Click **Associate**.

And that's it! When you return to your EC2 Instances page, you'll see that the new public IP is associated with the instance. You can now connect to your system using the new Elastic IP — but first, let's add our new IP to our active Security Group so that if we later attempt to connect through the VPN, we won't be blocked.

To open up your Security Group to the new IP:

1. From the AWS Management Console, select **Security Groups** from the left-hand pane.

2. Select the **VPN-WEB** security group we created, then tap **Actions > Inbound Rules**.

3. Add two new rules:

   - A **TCP Custom** rule for port 443 for **y.y.y.y/32**, where *y.y.y.y* is the Elastic IP you were assigned.
   - A **TCP Custom** Rule for port **80** for the same IP address and subnet mask.
   - A **TCP Custom** rule for port 22 for the same IP and subnet mask.

Why are we doing this? This will ensure that if you attempt to connect through your VPN to the web server a little later in our guide, you won't be blocked. If you recall, we opened up the following ports to our *home/ISP* address: 22, 80, 443, 1194 — but if we later attempt to connect to our web server *from* our VPN server given our current rule set, we'd be blocked. Adding the Elastic IP to our security group ensures that we can connect to ourselves!

> In order to streamline the install and configuration process, this guide assumes you're going to use a static IP, and not a domain name, for your VPN and web servers. We recommend running through the process with a static IP first, to get familiar with the process, and then you can either spin up a new instance and run through the process with your domain name after following the steps provided in *Assigning a Domain Name Using Amazon Route 53* on page 122 or regenerate your VPN and Apache certificates and keys with the new domain name. Because the process from beginning to end is straightforward and pretty fast, we recommend starting fresh with a new install — and it's good practice!

We are now ready to connect to the server and install OpenVPN!

4

Connecting to Your Server

To connect to your newly-launched server, you must obtain its external IP address. If you're still on the Amazon Web Service Launch Status page, click the instance ID link (it will start with an i-, followed by a series of 16 alphanumeric characters). If not, click **Services** in the top left corner, then click **EC2 > Running Instances.**

Select the server instance you just launched, and locate the **IPv4 Public IP** from either the top or bottom panes. It should be the same as the Elastic IP we just created. Select and copy the IP address to your clipboard and take a note of it for later.

- If you're using Linux or MacOS, see *Connecting to Your Server Using Linux or MacOS* on page 29 for login instructions.

- If you're using Windows, see *Connecting to your Server Using Windows* on page 30 for login instructions.

4.1   Connecting to Your Instance Using Linux or MacOS

1. Locate the key file you downloaded to your computer in the last chapter and run the following commands from a terminal or console window, where my-key.pem is the name of your key file and s.s.s.s is the IP address of the EC2 instance we just launched:

```
me@home:~$ chmod 700 my-key.pem

me@home:~$ ssh -i my-key.pem ec2-user@s.s.s.s
```

2. Type yes when prompted to continue connecting and jump forward to *Installing and Configuring OpenVPN Server* on page 35.

4.2   Connecting to Your Instance Using Windows

If you're a Windows user, you have a few more steps than the Linux and Mac users, unless you've enabled the Windows Subsystem for Linux (if so, open your terminal and use the instructions at *Connecting to Your Instance Using Linux or Mac OS)* on page 29. First, download and install PuTTY from the PuTTY download page at http://www.chiark.greenend.org.uk/~sgtatham/putty/latest.html .

In the following sections, we'll describe how to prepare your connection key for use with PuTTY.

Converting your .pem file to .ppk for Putty

Before connecting to your server with PuTTY, use PuTTYGen, installed with PuTTY, to convert your key pair into a format that PuTTY can understand.

To convert your key:

1. Tap inside the Windows Search box and type puttygen (or go to **Start** > **All Programs** > **PuTTY** > **PuTTYgen**). PuTTY Key Generator will open.

2. Under **Parameters**, select **RSA**.

3. Under **Actions**, click **Load**.

4. Navigate to the location you saved your key file, then click the down arrow next to **Putty Private Key Files (*.ppk)* and change it to** All Files (*.*)* to allow PuTTYgen to see your .pem file.

5. Select your file, then click **Open**. PuTTYgen will display a success message.

6. Click **OK** to dismiss the message and continue. Optionally, you can set a passphrase; this improves security but note that you'll need to use it each time you log on, which may make automation or file copying to the instance more difficult in the future. For the purposes of our quick setup, it shouldn't hinder, just a matter of personal choice (if you're on a shared computer, it may be a good idea to set a password).

7. Click **Save Private Key** and choose a location you'll remember, using the extension .ppk.

Connecting to Your Instance with PuTTY

Now that your key is converted, you're ready to create a session profile and connect!

1. Open the Putty application by clicking on the icon placed on your desktop at install or by typing Putty in the Start menu search window.

2. Click **Session** in the **Category** pane and type:

   `ec2-user@s.s.s.s`

   in the **Host** field, where s.s.s.s is the public IP address of your instance.

3. Keep the default connection type set to **SSH** and **Port** as 22. Then, from the **Category** pane, click **Connection**, then **SSH**, and then expand **Auth**.

4. Click **Browse**, navigate to and select your .ppk file, then click **Open**.

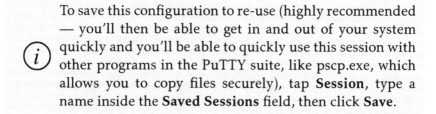

To save this configuration to re-use (highly recommended — you'll then be able to get in and out of your system quickly and you'll be able to quickly use this session with other programs in the PuTTY suite, like pscp.exe, which allows you to copy files securely), tap **Session**, type a name inside the **Saved Sessions** field, then click **Save**.

5. You should receive a message asking you to verify the server fingerprint. Review and accept it - and you're in!

Trouble logging in?

- Ensure that ec2-user precedes the host IP in PuTTY's **Host Name** field.

- Double-check that you generated a *private* key vs. *public* key in PuTTYGen.

- Check your EC2 security group to ensure that port 22 is open and your current IP is listed in the source field in *n.n.n.n/netmask* format (for example, 7.7.7.7/32 if your IP is 7.7.7.7.

5

Installing and Configuring OpenVPN Server

We chose OpenVPN as our VPN server because it's open source, popular, and well-supported. In fact, many of the more popular subscription-based VPN providers use OpenVPN, and client software exists for a large number of platforms. We'll be using version 2.4, the latest version as of publication.

Installing, configuring, and running OpenVPN server requires four basic steps:

- *Installing OpenVPN Server* on page 35: Install the software on your system.

- *Generating Authentication Credentials* on page 38: Generate the certificates and keys that clients exchange with the server to ensure secure communication.

- *Modifying Your VPN Server's Configuration* on page 43: Customize OpenVPN's default configuration for our deployment.

- *Forwarding Incoming Traffic to OpenVPN* on page 54: Configure your system to accept and forward incoming traffic to OpenVPN server.

5.1   Installing OpenVPN Server

We'll be installing OpenVPN 2.4.7, which is the latest available version in the stable 2.4 branch that contains all available security fixes. Because the version of OpenVPN available on the Amazon AMI is not the latest version, we'll be building our own installation file (rpm) from scratch. Don't worry — this is a lot faster and easier than it sounds!

Before we install, though, the first thing you'll want to do is bring your system up to date. Typically, when you first connect to an Amazon Linux AMI, you'll see a notification that system updates are available. This is because instances are created at a fixed point in time and updates are often released between the time the Amazon Linux AMI is built by the Amazon and CentOS teams and the time we launch it. The AMI also periodically checks for updates and modifies the motd, or message of the day, to let you know that there are updates to apply.

1. Update your system using the following command:

```
[ec2-user~]$ sudo yum -y update
```

-y is optional, but it allows you to skip confirmation to continue. It's a useful addition should you decide to automate these actions later. We'll also be running as root, using sudo for most of our installation commands. The ec2-user does not need to enter a password to obtain sudo access.

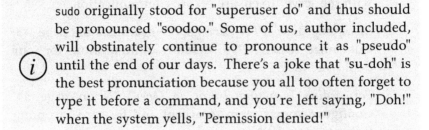

sudo originally stood for "superuser do" and thus should be pronounced "soodoo." Some of us, author included, will obstinately continue to pronounce it as "pseudo" until the end of our days. There's a joke that "su-doh" is the best pronunciation because you all too often forget to type it before a command, and you're left saying, "Doh!" when the system yells, "Permission denied!"

2. Next, we'll install some prerequisite software required to build OpenVPN's installable package (rpm) for CentOS. These packages include gcc, which is a C compiler that

builds the program, rpm-build, which we'll use to generate the rpm, and three additional packages OpenVPN depends on: openssl-devel (a software library used for encryption — we'll talk more about OpenSSL a bit later), lzo-devel (a library used for data compression), and pam-devel (libraries used for username/password authentication).

```
[ec2-user~]$ sudo yum -y install gcc rpm-build \
openssl-devel lzo-devel pam-devel
```

3. Download OpenVPN 2.4.7 source code:

```
[ec2-user~]$ wget https://swupdate.openvpn.org/community/
releases/openvpn-2.4.7.tar.gz
```

4. Use the rpmbuild utility to create an installable file:

```
[ec2-user~]$ rpmbuild -tb openvpn-2.4.7.tar.gz \
--with="enable-systemd"
```

5. Now we're ready to install OpenVPN 2.4:

```
[ec2-user~]$ sudo rpm -ivh \
rpmbuild/RPMS/x86_64/openvpn-2.4.7-1.x86_64.rpm
```

6. Next, add OpenVPN to system startup so that if the system is restarted, it starts automatically.

```
[ec2-user~]$ sudo chkconfig openvpn on
```

7. We'll also add OpenVPN as an "exclusion" to the system package manager. This is because we manually installed OpenVPN from its source and we want to update it ourselves — allowing OpenVPN to update automatically via the system can clobber parts of our installation.

First, open the yum configuration file, yum.conf:

```
[ec2-user~]$ sudo nano /etc/yum.conf
```

The nano and vi text editors are pre-installed on the Amazon Linux AMI; nano is great if you're new to Linux because its common commands are listed at the bottom of the editor window. If you have a favorite text editor, you can install it by running `yum -y install [editor-name]`.

8. At the bottom of the file, enter the following line and save and close the file:

```
exclude=openvpn
```

And that's it! OpenVPN is installed and we're ready to configure it.

5.2 Generating Authentication Credentials

Generating authentication credentials for your OpenVPN deployment is an important — probably the most important — part of your setup. Lucky for us, most of this is scripted and we can do everything we need with just a few commands. But before we start, let's quickly discuss what the commands we run will do.

In generating authentication credentials for our VPN server, we're going to build out our *public key infrastructure*, or PKI. PKI is the combination of applications, hardware, system components, processes, people, and policies we use to generate authentication credentials that allow components of a system to communicate securely.

Generally, a PKI will have a *Certificate Authority*, or CA, who acts as the "key-master." The CA has its own private key, which should be kept private, and a public certificate. It generates and signs both of these itself (or *self-signs*), because it's the *root* of the PKI.

Any entity that wants the CA to validate its identity will generate its own private and public key pair, and then will send the public key and its organization information to the CA in the form of a *certificate request*. The CA then verifies the information, and issues a digital certificate that certifies that the entity is verified and includes the CA's digital certificate. It's kind of like going to your state's Department of Motor Vehicles with your Social Security Card and some mail and leaving with your driver's license. In that case, your State is a bit like the Certificate Authority. (And like a State, the CA can revoke certificates as well as issue them.)

Issuing SSL certificates for installation on secure web sites is a common use of PKI. Say that you want to install an SSL certificate on your web site, so that users can access it using https. You generate a private and public key pair using the name of your web site and organization information, and then create a certificate request. You then upload that request to a root Certificate Authority, like Verisign. They verify that the keys match and then use some method to ensure you own the domain, and then they'll accept your payment and issue your certificate. When someone accesses your web site after you install the certificate, their browser checks your certificate against their own database of trusted CAs and a list of revoked certificates. If everything checks out, the user gets a little green lock on their browser that indicates your site is verified and secured using HTTPS (secure hypertext transfer protocol) implemented using TLS (Transport Layer Security), the cryptographic protocol used to encrypt the data you send to and receive from the secured web site.

The actual process of generating and signing these digital authentication files is done using a software library called OpenSSL (SSL is TLS' predecessor), which implements the cryptographic functions required to create public and private keys and certificates. It accepts generated keys and certificates as input and returns keys and certificates as we request them. Note that OpenSSL is an open implementation of SSL and TLS functions required to build our keystore and other implementations can be used with OpenVPN (PolarSSL is a popular option).

For our PKI, we'll create our own CA instead of using an external entity as certificate authority. We'll generate keys for our VPN server and clients and will request public certificates from our CA for each. We'll use a helper application, EasyRSA to generate these digital identity documents. EasyRSA wraps OpenSSL and allows us to quickly generate everything we need to build out our PKI with just a few simple commands. These public certificates will then be used by the VPN server and its clients to successfully identify and authenticate each other. When a client connects to the server, it passes its public key to the server, who compares the client's CA certificate with its own copy. Conversely, the server passes *its* public key to the client, who validates against its copy of the CA signature. If these match and the common name of the CA in the certificates matches up, both sides move forward to establish a connection and can exchange data freely.

We'll also create a TLS-authentication key, which is a static OpenVPN-specific key that both the client and server will share, to add an additional layer of security to the communications channel.

To generate your VPN server's authentication credentials:

1. Install `git` and clone the `easy-rsa` repository, which handles OpenVPN's default public key infrastructure:

```
[ec2-user~]$ sudo yum -y install git

[ec2-user~]$ git clone \
https://github.com/OpenVPN/easy-rsa.git
```

2. Move easyrsa3 out of its repository, copy it over to the OpenVPN installation directory, and clean up the project directory:

```
[ec2-user~]$ sudo cp -r easy-rsa/easyrsa3 \
/etc/openvpn/easy-rsa

[ec2-user~]$ rm -rf /home/ec2-user/easy-rsa
```

3. Move the sample variables file into an actual variables file:

```
[ec2-user~]$ cd /etc/openvpn/easy-rsa

[ec2-user~]$ sudo cp vars.example vars
```

4. Open vars with your favorite text editor:

```
[ec2-user~]$ sudo nano vars
```

5. Review the file, but don't change anything: leave the defaults.

For this deployment, we're going to use the default EASYRSA_KEY_SIZE set in vars, 2048 bits. If you set your key size to 4096 bits, it can take a few hours to generate your Diffie-Hellman parameters on a virtual machine that's just booted up, so it's a good idea to stick to 2048 bits the first time you do this. 2048 bit keys are secure (NIST and RSA have estimated that 2048 bit keys should be sufficient through 2030, so they have a good bit of life left in them). Just don't use 1024 — it's not secure!

If you decide to future-proof your installation with a 4096-bit key, it's a good idea to generate your keys on real hardware. You'll speed up key generation and, the more randomness you introduce into the key, the stronger it will be. This randomness is called *entropy*, which is data that your crypto application uses while generating a key in order to increase its randomness and thus its security. Therefore, a system where you've got a number of windows open, are alt-tabbing through windows, and using the mouse will generate a stronger key faster than a key generated on a predictable cloud-based virtual machine that hasn't been running very long, isn't doing very many unpredictable things, and isn't very unique at its core from any of the other virtual machines around it.

There are a number of tricks people try to speed up key generation on VMs — but nothing compares with mad alt-tabbing and frenetic mousing on a busy workstation that hasn't been rebooted in a good, long while!

Let's build our certificate authority, server, and client certificates and keys:

1. Run the following to initiate your Public Key Infrastructure, or PKI, datastore:

```
[ec2-user~]$ sudo ./easyrsa init-pki
```

2. Run `build-ca`, which generates the Certificate Authority (CA) private and public keys that will then in turn be used to generate server and client keys for OpenVPN.

```
[ec2-user~]$ sudo ./easyrsa build-ca nopass
```

The `nopass` option will skip setting a passphrase. One reason to avoid a passphrase here and when building the server is that it's required during startup. If you want OpenVPN to start up without user interaction after a system reboot interaction (or without placing the password somewhere insecurely on your system), it's best to build the CA with nopass.

3. When prompted, enter the address of your server as the CA's **Common Name** and press Enter. This should match your server IP or domain name you use to connect to the system. In our case, this will be the Elastic IP we set up. If you're using a domain name you've already configured as described in Assigning a Domain Name Using Amazon Route 53, you would use that name here.

4. Next, we'll generate our VPN server private key, public key, and certificate (you can technically use any name in place of server, but leave it as "server" for ease of running through the exercise):

```
[ec2-user~]$ sudo ./easyrsa build-server-full server nopass
```

5. Next, we'll generate our Diffie-Hellman parameters, which are used for encryption on the server side of the VPN:

```
[ec2-user~]$ sudo ./easyrsa gen-dh
```

Take a break! This step can take about ten minutes. Or, if you're feeling like a superstar, open another terminal window and jump forward to *Configuring Apache HTTP Server to Serve Client Credentials* on page 57 to set up your Apache web server while you wait. Just remember to come back here to generate your client keys.

6. Next, we'll generate a key pair that can be used for clients we want to connect to the VPN. We're just going to create one set here that can be used by multiple clients and users. If you want to use unique client credentials for each user, you can come back and build them later using the same procedure, but with different names in place of client. This option also allows for a passphrase.

```
[ec2-user~]$ sudo ./easyrsa build-client-full client nopass
```

7. To further secure the system, we'll generate a TLS Authentication key to further secure the communications channel and protect against denial-of-service attacks:

```
[ec2-user~]$ sudo openvpn --genkey --secret ta.key
```

And that's it — your key infrastructure is complete and you're ready to customize your server configuration.

5.3 Modifying Your VPN Server's Configuration

If a VPN server is not properly configured, it may not send DNS server configurations or routes directly to clients — causing your DNS queries to travel over the open Internet, outside your tunnel. This is what you'll see referred to as *DNS Leakage*. You'll also hear the term *IPv6 leakage* talked about

43

regarding improperly-configured VPN servers. In the past, most devices have typically used IPv4 addresses; IPv4 is an acronym for Internet Protocol version 4, where network addresses are represented by a series of four numbers separated by dots — 127.0.0.1, for example (although, strictly speaking, 127.0.0.1 is not technically a network address; it's what's referred to as a *loopback* address; it's how every system refers to itself: the "me" of IP addresses. You'll also see this referred to as "localhost").

IPv6, or Internet Protocol version 6, was created because IPv4 was quickly running out of address space. It's been in development since the 1990s and started to be practically implemented in the early 2000s. It's got a much bigger address space than IPv4. For example, the loopback address 127.0.0.1 in IPv4 is 0000:0000:0000:0000:0000:0000:0000:0001 in IPv6 (or ::1 in IPv6 shorthand) — that's a lot of address space and we're now ready for every toaster, coffee maker, and even toothbrush to phone home! (Yikes!)

Most network devices now are considered "dual-stack" meaning they support both IPv4 *and* IPv6 connections. Apple devices now use pure IPv6 natively. However, a lot of VPN servers don't support IPv6 connections (even if the underlying VPN software does support it, as OpenVPN does).

In this case, these VPN servers will still handle IPv6 requests, even if they route them to IPv4 locations — if they don't, clients send the requests elsewhere, "leaking" requests outside of the VPN tunnel.

For our deployment, we're using Amazon EC2 instances that do not support IPv6 out-of-the-box, but we'll still have to handle these requests to ensure our clients' traffic stays secure.

So, as you see, correct configuration is important! We'll add all of our configuration options to a file called server.conf, but note that OpenVPN will use any file with a .conf extension located at /etc/openvpn/ on the system. For this reason, it's really important to only have one .conf file in the directory. If you have more than one, it will attempt to run all instances it sees and will fail.

Tip: To search through your command history on Linux, which allows you to quickly re-type any command you've previously typed, press CTRL-R and type any portion of the command to recall it. If you want to clear your history at any time, log out, log back in, and clear the information in the ~/.bash_history file (this is shorthand for the home directory, and in our case on EC2, would resolve to /home/ec2-user/.bash_history).

Parameters in OpenVPN configuration files are specified by the parameter name followed by its value. Comments are delimited by # and disabled parameters are prefaced with a semi-colon (;).

We'll use a sample file to get started.

1. Copy the sample configuration file from OpenVPN's sample files directory into the OpenVPN directory:

```
[ec2-user~]$ sudo cp  /usr/share/doc/openvpn-2.4.7/sample/\
sample-config-files/server.conf /etc/openvpn/
```

2. Let's open server.conf and take a look:

```
[ec2-user~]$ sudo nano /etc/openvpn/server.conf
```

The first option you see, ;local a.b.c.d, is disabled. It indicates which local IP to listen to. This would be the eth0 inet address you see when you type ifconfig from the command line — an address typically in the 172.0.0.0 address block. Because we only have a single interface connected to the outside world, we can leave this option commented out; the server will figure out which interface to bind to. If you were using a system with multiple network-connected interfaces, you would explicitly set this.

We'll also keep the port and proto (protocol) options the same for this exercise. Note that you can change these and may have very good reasons for doing so — just be sure to change your Amazon Security Group to allow you to access the port and protocol you choose and that you don't plan to run other services on those ports. In previous versions of OpenVPN, you had to add udp6 or tcp6 (depending on which protocol you chose) to ensure that ipv6 traffic was forwarded through the tunnel. In OpenVPN, this option is no longer necessary.

Why would one consider changing the port and protocol?
It depends on your needs. UDP is fast, but lossy, because
it's *stateless*. TCP is a little slower, but more reliable,
because it's *stateful*. To simplify it, take a scenario where
you've got to get two buckets of golf balls thrown over a
fence. You're required to throw all of the balls in your
first bucket, but you've got to wait for someone on the
other side to acknowledge that they picked up each ball
before you throw the next: that's TCP traffic. It's slower,
but the person on the other side didn't miss a ball. For
the second bucket, you're allowed to toss ball after ball
without acknowledgment. You can throw the balls faster,
but a few might end up in the bushes: that's UDP traffic.

Another consideration might be that if your ISP is
blocking, throttling or "shaping" UDP traffic on certain
ports, TCP 443 may be a good choice because it looks
just like regular https traffic. For this guide, however,
we recommend *not* setting your VPN to TCP 443 as we're
going to be setting up a secure web server further on
to serve your OpenVPN client configuration files. It's
also uncommon for ISPs to block VPN traffic on default
UDP ports because of their ubiquitous use in business
(although I have seen private networks do this and was
able to bring up a new VPN with TCP on port 80 to get
around it).

The great thing about being able to control and launch
your own VPN server quickly is that you can change the
port whenever you want or need to, you just have to
restart the server and update your client configuration.

3. After the port and protocol options, you'll see an option
to choose the type of network behavior you want — you
can choose from tun or tap — we'll keep the default. tun
configures an interface that allows clients to connect
through the VPN to the outside world, but not to other

VPN users. If you were to choose tap, the VPN interface is bridged and users could also then connect to each other — neat, but not what we want right now (you'd also have to configure a few more routing options). We will, however, add an entry to create an IPv6 tunnel, tun-ipv6 and an instruction to push the information down to the client push tun-ipv6.

```
# "dev tun" will create a routed IP tunnel,
# "dev tap" will create an ethernet tunnel.
# Use "dev tap0" if you are ethernet bridging
# and have precreated a tap0 virtual interface
# and bridged it with your ethernet interface.
# If you want to control access policies
# over the VPN, you must create firewall
# rules for the the TUN/TAP interface.
# On non-Windows systems, you can give
# an explicit unit number, such as tun0.
# On Windows, use "dev-node" for this.
# On most systems, the VPN will not function
# unless you partially or fully disable
# the firewall for the TUN/TAP interface.
;dev tap
dev tun
```

4. We *must* change the location of our CA certificate, the server's certificate and private key, and the certificate the server uses to encrypt its connection (note that the file specifies dh2048.pem; we'll be changing that to dh.pem):

```
# Any X509 key management system can be used.
# OpenVPN can also use a PKCS #12 formatted key file
# (see "pkcs12" directive in man page).

ca /etc/openvpn/easy-rsa/pki/ca.crt
cert /etc/openvpn/easy-rsa/pki/issued/server.crt
key /etc/openvpn/easy-rsa/pki/private/server.key # This file \
# should be kept secret

# Diffie hellman parameters.
# Generate your own with:
# openssl dhparam -out dh2048.pem 2048

dh /etc/openvpn/easy-rsa/pki/dh.pem
```

5. Next, we'll skip down to the `server` option. We'll leave the default for IPv4 connection, and add one additional entry for IPv6:

```
# Configure server mode and supply a VPN subnet
# for OpenVPN to draw client addresses from.
# The server will take 10.8.0.1 for itself,
# the rest will be made available to clients.
# Each client will be able to reach the server
# on 10.8.0.1. Comment this line out if you are
# ethernet bridging. See the man page for more info.

server 10.8.0.0 255.255.255.0
ifconfig-ipv6 2001:db8:0:123::1 2001:db8:0:123::2
```

6. Next, scroll way down to uncomment push `redirect-gateway def1 bypass-dhcp` by removing the semicolon (;) from the beginning *and* add an option for IPv6. These options push down a directive to clients that forces them to redirect *all* of their traffic through the VPN. If you're supporting iOS devices that haven't yet been updated to 10.x, the push `"redirect-gateway ipv6"` option is essential as there's a bug in iOS 9.x where all IPv6 traffic (for iOS 9.x, that's *all* traffic because iOS 9.x and higher run a full IPv6 stack) will travel outside the VPN tunnel if the IPv6 gateway is not redirected to the VPN. This is fixed in iOS 10.x, so you can omit this directive if all iPhones the VPN is serving are updated.

```
push "redirect-gateway def1 bypass-dhcp"
push "redirect-gateway ipv6"  # Only necessary if \
#supporting iOS 9.x clients
push "route-ipv6 2001:db8:0:abc::/64"
push "route-ipv6 2000::/3"
```

7. Uncomment the following values by removing the semicolon (;) from the beginning of each statement and updating the DNS entries to the DNS servers you want pushed down to clients (if you want to use OpenDNS, use these entries in their entirety, if you want to use Google, use 8.8.8.8 and 8.8.4.4 and so on). You can add additional lines if your have more than two favored DNS servers:

```
push "dhcp-option DNS 208.67.222.222"
push "dhcp-option DNS 208.67.220.220"
```

Note that pushing DNS servers down to clients won't work for all clients in all situations; for example, on Mac OS using Tunnelblick, the user's manually-set DNS will always override DNS entries pushed down by the server.

8. Uncomment `duplicate-cn`. This is important if you plan to connect with more than one device using the same certificate.

```
# IF YOU HAVE NOT GENERATED INDIVIDUAL
# CERTIFICATE/KEY PAIRS FOR EACH CLIENT,
# EACH HAVING ITS OWN UNIQUE "COMMON NAME",
# UNCOMMENT THIS LINE OUT.
duplicate-cn
```

9. Make sure that `tls-auth ta.key 0` is uncommented and set the location of `ta.key` file we created (/etc/openvpn/easy-rsa). This adds additional security to our connection and protects against Denial-of-Service attacks and port floods. The client configuration will get a similar line, with a 1 instead of a 0 (but no location for the key is used in the client configuration; the key is embedded in the client configuration file).

```
tls-auth /etc/openvpn/easy-rsa/ta.key 0
```

10. In the cipher section, keep the default AES-256-CBC:

```
# Select a cryptographic cipher.
# This config item must be copied to
# the client config file as well.
# Note that v2.4 client/server will automatically
# negotiate AES-256-GCM in TLS mode.
# See also the ncp-cipher option in the manpage
cipher AES-256-CBC
```

 To view a list of ciphers supported by your version of OpenVPN, run `openvpn -show-ciphers`.

11. The next section contains compression options. If you plan to use ChromeOS clients, keep this commented out. It will only work with 2.4 OpenVPN clients and ChromeOS OpenVPN versions commonly lag far behind. You can enable `comp-lzo` if you plan to support older versions of OpenVPN clients.

12. You can optionally control the maximum number of clients that can connect with the `max-clients` option. The default is 100.

13. Uncomment the following lines, which tell OpenVPN to drop privileges from root to the nobody user after it starts up (it needs root privileges for networking setup and breakdown). This is a good basic security measure for any process you run — in the event that the OpenVPN process is exploited, it will provide an attacker fewer system privileges.

```
user nobody
group nobody
```

51

These options work for the CentOS-based system we use in this guide or any Red Hat Enterprise Linux-based system. If you're using these instructions on a Debian or Debian-based OS like Ubuntu, change group nobody to group nogroup.

14. Next, we'll add a few additional lines to force the server to use a little higher-level security than its defaults. We'll set the TLS version minimum to 1.2 to ensure clients don't connect with a lower version and will set OpenVPN's message authentication (HMAC) to SHA256 (in testing without these options, clients have been observed connecting with TLS 1.1, with HMAC using SHA1 — so let's force the issue). You can add this anywhere in the file:

```
tls-version-min 1.2
auth SHA256
```

15. Next, we'll add a list of TLS ciphers that can be used. This restricts how clients can connect and ensures they connect using the strongest ciphers available to both sides.

```
tls-cipher TLS-ECDHE-RSA-WITH-AES-256-GCM-SHA384:TLS-ECDHE-
ECDSA-WITH-AES-256-GCM-SHA384:TLS-ECDHE-RSA-WITH-AES-256-
CBC-SHA384:TLS-DHE-RSA-WITH-AES-256-GCM-SHA384:TLS-DHE-RSA-
WITH-AES-256-CBC-SHA
```

You can see a list of all TLS ciphers available by running openvpn --show-tls.

16. After you've made your changes, save and close the file. Without all of the comments and blank lines. You can run this fun command:

```
sudo sed -e '/^\s*#.*$/d' -e '/^\s*$/d' -e '/^;/d' \
/etc/openvpn/server.conf
```

It will get you the same output and should look something like the following:

```
port 1194
proto udp
dev tun
ca /etc/openvpn/easy-rsa/pki/ca.crt
cert /etc/openvpn/easy-rsa/pki/issued/server.crt
key /etc/openvpn/easy-rsa/pki/private/server.key
dh /etc/openvpn/easy-rsa/pki/dh.pem
server 10.8.0.0 255.255.255.0
ifconfig-ipv6 2001:db8:0:123::1 2001:db8:0:123::2
ifconfig-pool-persist ipp.txt
push "redirect-gateway def1 bypass-dhcp"
push "redirect-gateway ipv6"  # Only necessary if
  # supporting iOS 9.x clients
push "route-ipv6 2001:db8:0:abc::/64"
push "route-ipv6 2000::/3"
push "dhcp-option DNS 208.67.222.222"
push "dhcp-option DNS 208.67.220.220"
duplicate-cn
keepalive 10 120
tls-auth /etc/openvpn/easy-rsa/ta.key 0
cipher AES-256-CBC
user nobody
group nobody
persist-key
persist-tun
status openvpn-status.log
verb 3
explicit-exit-notify 1
tls-version-min 1.2
auth SHA256
tls-cipher TLS-ECDHE-RSA-WITH-AES-256-GCM-SHA384:TLS-
ECDHE-ECDSA-WITH-AES-256-GCM-SHA384:TLS-ECDHE-RSA-WITH-
AES-256-CBC-SHA384:TLS-DHE-RSA-WITH-AES-256-GCM-SHA384:
TLS-DHE-RSA-WITH-AES-256-CBC-SHA
```

You're now ready to update your server's network configuration to allow VPN traffic to pass through it!

5.4 Forwarding Incoming Traffic to OpenVPN

Now that we've got authentication credentials set and our server configured, we're ready to put it all together to allow traffic to flow through the system.

To update your system's routing to allow traffic to pass through:

1. We'll first change the system's `net.ipv4.ip_forward` setting.

   Because the system won't allow us to edit the file in place even as `root`, we'll create a temporary file, then move it over to a spot where it will get picked up by the system. Once set, this will allow the system to pass network traffic from network interface to network interface (in our case, the physical connection to the outside world, eth0, and our virtual tunnel interface (tun0):

   ```
   [ec2-user~]$ sudo echo "net.ipv4.ip_forward = 1" >> \
   /tmp/11-sysctl.conf


   [ec2-user~]$ sudo mv /tmp/11-sysctl.conf \
   /etc/sysctl.d/11-sysctl.conf
   ```

2. Run `sysctl` to implement the change:

   ```
   [ec2-user~]$ sudo sysctl --system
   ```

   You can verify this is set correctly to 1 by using the following command:

   ```
   [ec2-user~]$ sudo sysctl -a |grep ip_forward
   ```

3. Next, we'll set up our internal VPN network using `firewalld` and save and apply our changes:

   ```
   [ec2-user~]$ sudo yum -y install firewalld
   [ec2-user~]$ sudo systemctl enable firewalld
   [ec2-user~]$ sudo systemctl start firewalld
   [ec2-user~]$ sudo firewall-cmd --zone=public --add-service \
   openvpn --permanent
   [ec2-user~]$ sudo firewall-cmd --add-masquerade --permanent
   [ec2-user~]$ sudo firewall-cmd --reload
   ```

Because we add openvpn as a service, any port it attempts to open will be allowed by `firewalld`. You can check that the services are successfully enabled by running `sudo firewall-cmd --list-services`.

4. You're ready to start your VPN server!

```
[ec2-user-]$ sudo systemctl start openvpn
```

And that's it for now for the server side! OpenVPN should start up successfully. If not, check `/var/log/messages` for errors (run `sudo tail -f /var/log/messages` to see the last messages (type `CTRL+C` to exit the tail session) or `sudo cat /var/log/messages` to display the full file). With `systemctl`, you can also type `sudo systemctl status openvpn` to check status.

Note that sometimes, if you've got a configuration error and OpenVPN didn't start successfully, attempting to restart after fixing your issue via `sudo systemctl start openvpn` fails silently with no real clue as to what's happening in the logs. Not sure why this is, but if you explicitly stop it again with `sudo systemctl stop openvpn` and start again and it should spin up successfully.

You can go back into `/etc/openvpn/server.conf` and change the logging location and logging level (`verb`) if needed. The default logging level is 3, but it can go up to 9; 5 is a reasonable level for most debugging.

Now, we'll quickly set up a secure web site using Apache HTTP Server to use to securely transmit our client credentials from our VPN server to the devices we want to connect to our VPN.

6

Configuring Apache HTTP Server to Serve Client Credentials

Historically, getting your client VPN configuration files, which use private keys, over to your phone securely has been tricky. The standard advice is usually to connect your phone to your computer, fire up iTunes (for iPhone) or mount your SD card (Android) and manually copy the file over. That's not super user friendly, and it's absolutely not fast.

It sounds crazy to install and configure a secure Web server *just* to serve your VPN configuration file...but what's another five minutes vs. plugging your iPhone into iTunes and waiting for sync before you can copy files over? It's actually faster to spin up a secure web server, and it's good experience that you can transfer to other projects.

Because we're setting this system up *just* to serve our VPN configuration files and we're going to keep it locked down, we'll spin it up from the same server. For sensitive installations, you might want to use a separate server.

Let's install and configure Apache HTTP server to serve our configuration files:

1. After logging into your EC2 instance, install Apache HTTP server, httpd:

   ```
   [ec2-user~]$ sudo yum -y install httpd
   ```

2. Optionally, if you want your web server to kick on when your system starts, add httpd to startup, so that if the system is restarted, it starts automatically.

```
[ec2-user~]$ sudo systemctl enable httpd
```

3. Start httpd:

```
[ec2-user~]$ sudo systemctl start httpd
```

4. Open up the internal firewall so that we can access our web server. We'll add the secure port for https, 443, while we're at it:

```
[ec2-user~]$ sudo firewall-cmd --zone=public --add-service \
http --permanent

[ec2-user~]$ sudo firewall-cmd --zone=public --add-service \
https --permanent

[ec2-user~]$ sudo firewall-cmd --reload
```

Now, when you run sudo firewall-cmd --list-all, the output should look like the following:

```
[ec2-user~]$ sudo firewall-cmd --list-all
public
target: default
icmp-block-inversion: no
interfaces:
sources:
services: ssh dhcpv6-client http openvpn https
ports:
protocols:
masquerade: yes
forward-ports:
source-ports:
icmp-blocks:
rich rules:
```

5. Test your basic install: From your browser, open http://s.s.s.s/, where s.s.s.s is the public IP of your system.

That was quick — you should see an Amazon AMI Apache HTTP Server test page. You've successfully installed a basic web server. If the page does not open, check your Security Group settings from the Amazon Web Services Management Console to ensure that there is an incoming HTTP (port 80) rule configured with your IP/32 as the source. While you're there, make sure you've got one for HTTPS (port 443) open for yourself, too.

6. Now, lct's enable https on our server. Install mod_ssl, the TLS/SSL module for Apache HTTP Server.

```
[ec2-user~] sudo yum -y install mod_ssl
```

6.1   Installing Server Certificates for Apache

Next, we'll generate a certificate the server will use to encrypt traffic it sends and receives. We'll create a self-signed certificate for this purpose.

This allows us to use TLS encryption without having to go to a commercial Certificate Authority.   Since our web server is personal and likely ephemeral (we don't know how long we'll keep it up, we might bring it down after a few hours and build something else), we don't really need to be verified by any "authority" but ourselves. Because *we* are the CA in this case, we have control of the private key. Also, you can't get an CA-signed certificate for an IP address, they are only issued for domains (we'll get into obtaining a domain and obtaining CA-signed certificates a little later).

This does result in browser warnings when you attempt to connect to the system because the browser doesn't recognize your CA. But no worries, your connection is secure, it's just that the browser doesn't recognize your CA as a sanctioned root CA. You can import your CA's certificate into your browser to clear these warnings if you like, as we'll discuss in *Configuring Browsers to Accept Your Self-Signed Certificate* on page 67.

If you intend to deploy your web server to a larger and/or more public audience, you can obtain a certificate from a certificate authority and follow their instructions for generating a certificate request and placing the resulting data on the server. We, however, are just quickly creating a private depot for secure file drops for our own use and not for the general public, so a self-signed certificate is fast, easy, secure, and sufficient for our use case.

To generate your server's private key and public certificate:

1. Log into your system and run the following command:

```
[ec2-user~]$ sudo openssl req -new -newkey rsa:4096 \
-sha256 -days 365 -nodes -x509 -keyout \
/etc/pki/tls/private/localhost.key -out \
/etc/pki/tls/certs/localhost.crt
```

This command generates a key and certificate pair that expires in one year. You can make the days value smaller or larger, depending on your needs. You can also change the RSA key size (rsa:nnn). For our purposes, because this is a single personal server and we're not concerned about a little extra computational power here and there, we set this to 4096, but 2048 is also an acceptable value — the larger the key, the more computation required when you connect.

Why are we generating a 4096-bit key here when we didn't for OpenVPN? It's purely a matter of impatience: generating a regular old 4096-bit key on a VM is *a lot* faster than generating 4096-bit Diffie-Hellman parameters.

With this command, the server's private key, localhost.key, and certificate, localhost.crt, are placed in the directories Apache will look for them. The key file should be protected at all costs — if a nefarious actor obtains it, they can impersonate your server. The certificate file, however, is public, and can be sent to anyone you want to access your system. Once installed in their browser or keystore, they'll be able to connect to your web server without browser warnings.

2. When prompted, provide the information requested. All fields are optional *except* the **Common Name** and it's very important that you set the Common Name (CN) to match exactly what anyone attempting to connect to the server will use to connect. For example, if our publicly-accessible IP was 3.3.3.3, we'd set it to 3.3.3.3. If we were planning on configuring a domain name for a more permanent setup and accessing it via test.diy-vpn.com, we would set test.diy-vpn.com as the CN.

3. Restart the web service:

```
[ec2-user~]$ sudo systemctl restart httpd
```

4. Now, try to open `https://s.s.s.s/`, where `s.s.s.s` is the IP address of your Apache server.

5. The page should load a browser warning that indicates that the certificate authority is not valid. Because we know we're connecting to a resource we control, click **Advanced > Proceed Anyway** (or **Accept the Risk and Continue**).

If you're using the server as a one-off and not bothered by proceeding through the browser error, you're almost done!

If you plan to use your Web server for more than one-off VPN configuration hand-offs, refer to *Configuring Browsers to Accept Your Self-Signed Certificate* on page 67 after you've finished configuring the server. It's a good idea to do this if you're planning on using the web server for any length of time — that way, you'll be alerted by your browser if the server identity changes, indicating that your connection may be intercepted.

If you plan to share your VPN credentials with others, you may want to set up a domain name for the server as described in *Assigning a Domain Name Using Amazon Route 53* on page 122 and getting a real SSL certificate from *Installing an SSL Certificate with LetsEncrypt* on page 125.

Because we're planning on using this server to transmit our client configuration files, which contains the client's private key, we need to configure a few more items to ensure there's no data leakage and to configure our web server properties so that our phones' file systems understand what to do with the OpenVPN client configuration file formats (.ovpn and .onc files).

6.2 Configuring Your Secure Web Server to Serve VPN Configuration Files

Now that we've got our secure site up and running, we want to be sure that we don't accidentally goof up and send data unencrypted by opening `http://host_address` instead of `https://host_address`. There are a few ways you can do this. You can block port 80 altogether, but that's suboptimal — if you send the link to someone, they may just enter the URL without the protocol (http vs. https) and it won't load at all. The more elegant way of handling this is to redirect from the non-secure site to the secure site.

To configure your web server to serve configuration files:

1. On the server, open `/etc/httpd/conf/httpd.conf` with a text editor:

   ```
   [ec2-user~]$ sudo nano /etc/httpd/conf/httpd.conf
   ```

2. Locate the **ServerName** option near the top of the file. Uncomment it by removing the #, and replace `www.example.com:80` with your public IP (if you're running through this procedure again after configuring a domain name, use the domain name here instead). No need to keep the :80, just the host itself will suffice.

3. Scroll down to the bottom of the file and enter the following, where *host_address* is your server address or domain name:

```
<VirtualHost *:80>
  ServerName host_address
  Redirect / https://host_address/
</VirtualHost>
<VirtualHost *:443>
  ServerName host_address
</VirtualHost>
```

For our example, this would be the public IP address of our web server. If you set up a domain name as described in *Assigning a Domain Name Using Amazon Route 53* on page 122, this would be the system's host name — for example, diy-vpn.com.

4. Next, add the following lines to add a bit of extra security — these stop Apache from sending its version number and installed modules to lookie-loos, and sets headers to transmit a message that tells web crawlers not to index your pages:

```
ServerSignature Off
ServerTokens Prod
Header set X-Robots-Tag "noindex"
```

These options aren't strictly necessary if you are planning to continue to restrict access to the outside world, but they don't hurt — and are good general practice. Providing version numbers and installed modules on demand makes a hacker's job easier: If you know the software version, you can pick an exploit that will work against it much faster.

5. Next, add some information to show web browsers how to handle VPN configuration files (this is especially important for ChromeOS, as it will download a 0 byte file unless we do this):

```
<IfModule headers_module>
  <FilesMatch ".(ovpn|onc)$">
    Header Set Content-type application/x-openvpn-profile
  </FilesMatch>
</IfModule>
```

What do these lines do? First, we're looking for files that have an `ovpn` extension. If that matches, we tell the browser that the file should not be rendered as text, but instead should be associated with the OpenVPN application. In testing, desktop operating systems seem to ignore the content type, but iPhones and Androids happily just "get it" because the OpenVPN app registers its filetype with the phone OS when you install it.

6. Save and close the file and restart your web server:

```
[ec2-user~]$ sudo systemctl restart httpd
```

If you receive any errors here or restart fails, check the log for hints (`sudo cat /var/log/httpd/error_log` or check httpd service status with `sudo systemctl status httpd.service`).

7. From your browser, load your site using the web address (`http://host_address/`, where `host_address` is your site's static IP). The site should redirect automatically to `https://host_address`, so you can verify that worked. If the server doesn't load, check to make sure your Amazon Security Group is configured correctly:

- Fire up your browser and navigate to the AWS Management Console (https://aws.amazon.com), sign in, select **EC2** and then click **Security Groups**.

- Select the Security Group you associated with your Apache Web Server, then tap **Actions > Edit inbound rules**. Add two new TCP rules: One for port 80 and one for port 443. For the Source, we recommend just putting your own IP here, or the IPs of hosts you plan to serve client config files to. Note that AWS requires CIDR notation, so for a single IP, you'd use y.y.y.y/32, for a range of 256 IPs in a subnet between y.y.y.0-y.y.y.255, you'd use y.y.y.y/24.

Once you've verified you can access your web server, you're ready to password-protect your download directory.

6.3   Password-protecting Your Download Directory

Let's add a password to our download directory. While our current Amazon Security Group configuration doesn't allow *anyone* from the outside world to access our server yet, you may want or need to open up access to a wider audience at some point — for example, if you want to set your parents up on your VPN and they're on the road using a mobile device whose IP will change as they travel.

This will ensure that only those who know the username and password can access the files inside. We'll create a subdirectory for downloads, and protect it with digest authentication for a username and password we provide.

1. From your AWS instance, create a new directory and give the apache user ownership of the file:

   ```
   [ec2-user~]$ sudo mkdir /var/www/html/downloads && \
   sudo chown -R apache:apache /var/www/html/downloads
   ```

2. Type the following, where vpn is the username you want for downloaders and vpnweb is the "realm," which is used to further encrypt the password (you can use a different name for your realm; the only stipulation is that it must also match the realm we specify in the web server configuration file a few steps from now):

   ```
   [ec2-user~]$ sudo htdigest -c /etc/httpd/.digestauth \
   vpnweb vpn
   ```

   This generates a password file named .digestauth which contains a list of usernames and passwords that will be allowed to access your download directory. You can name the file whatever you'd like, just be sure to remember it (as well as the realm and user name).

3. When prompted to enter a password, enter it (and remember it! But if you do forget it later, just come back and rerun the previous step — without the `-c`, as the `-c` option creates the file — and restart httpd).

4. Optionally, to add new users, you can type `sudo htdigest /etc/httpd/.digestauth vpnweb new-user` where `new-user` is the user name you want to use.

5. When you display the file (`sudo cat /etc/httpd/.digestauth`), it should look something like this:

   ```
   vpn:downloaders:e00883e6cdbd8dc9ee609d5c99e920bf
   ```

6. Change ownership on your password file:

   ```
   [ec2-user~]$ sudo chown apache:apache \
   /etc/httpd/.digestauth
   ```

7. Open `/etc/httpd/conf/httpd.conf` with a text editor and paste the following lines in (you can place them at the end of the file or after the last `</Directory>` tag you see. Either is fine).

   ```
   <Directory "/var/www/html/downloads">
     AuthType Digest
     AuthName "vpnweb"
     AuthUserFile /etc/httpd/.digestauth
     Require valid-user
   </Directory>
   ```

8. Restart the web server:

   ```
   [ec2-user~]$ sudo systemctl restart httpd
   ```

9. Verify everything works by popping open a browser and attempting to access `https://host_address/` (this should work without asking for a password) and then `https://host_address/downloads` (this should require a username and password).

Initially, you'll see a browser warning because we're using self-signed certificates to secure our connection. The connection is secure, but because we issued the security certificate ourselves, the browser can't authenticate it against its list of approved and official certificate authorities. If these warnings bother you, proceed to the next section for detailed information about setting up trust between your browser and your secure server (and it's pretty gratifying to see the happy green lock of safety when you're attached to a system you deployed yourself, let's be honest!).

If this doesn't matter so much to you and you want to connect to your VPN as soon as possible, skip forward to *Configuring Client Connections to OpenVPN Server* on page 73 (or jump back to step 6 in *Installing OpenVPN* on page 43 if you ran through this procedure while waiting for your OpenVPN Diffie-Hellman keys to generate!).

6.4 Configuring Browsers to Accept Your Self-Signed Certificate

While you can live with angry browser warnings about self-signed certificates for one-off use when downloading a configuration file or two in a hurry, you may want to get rid of the warnings if you plan to use the site for more than a speedy download.

Luckily, it's quick and easy to install your server certificate locally to avoid warnings in the future. It's also important to tip you off in the event that your connection is compromised — because let's face it, very few people compare signatures every time they click **Proceed Anyway**, and it's better to be safe than sorry to avoid a man-in-the-middle situation, where an attacker is attempting to impersonate your server to intercept your communications.

If you don't plan on using your web server to download VPN credentials more than once or twice, you can skip straight to *Configuring Clients* on page 73. Or, if you do intend to use the web server for other purposes, you can choose to register a domain and get a real SSL certificate to secure the site. For instructions, see *Registering a Domain Name with Route 53* on 122 and the sections that follow it.

Ensuring that the browser trusts your certificate is especially important if you're sharing your VPN connection with a family member or friend — under no circumstances do you want to train them to automatically click Proceed Anyway when presented with a certificate error.

The first thing you'll want to do is download the server's public certificate to your device. And hey, look at that, we have already have a secure way to pass it around! Note that there's very little danger in passing your public certificate around — you can send it to others you want to access your server safely, but *never do this with your private key*. The key file should remain locked away and safe, and never transmitted over an unencrypted connection.

You can skip the following procedure if you're using Firefox. Firefox can fetch the certificate directly from the server when you add an exception for it. See *Installing a Server Certificate on Mozilla Firefox* on page 69 for instructions and caveats.

1. On the Apache server, copy the certificate to the web root and change its ownership to user/group apache:

```
[ec2-user~]$ sudo cp /etc/pki/tls/certs/localhost.crt \
/var/www/html/downloads/

[ec2-user~]$ sudo chown apache:apache \
/var/www/html/downloads/localhost.crt
```

2. Open your browser to https://s.s.s.s/downloads/ localhost.crt, where s.s.s.s is your system's public IP. Log in using the credentials you set up earlier, then download and save the certificate as a .crt file.

3. On the Apache server, delete the certificate from your web root when you're done:

```
[ec2-user~]$ sudo rm /var/www/html/localhost.crt
```

Next, you'll want to install the certificate on your system. Use the sections that follow for instructions specific to your browser:

- *Installing a Server Certificate on Google Chrome* on page 69

- *Installing a Server Certificate on Mozilla Firefox* on page 69

- *Installing a Server Certificate on MacOS Safari* on page 70

Installing a Server Certificate on Google Chrome

You can add the server certificate directly to Chrome's certificate store and it will trust the server until you delete or revoke the certificate.

1. In Chrome, type **chrome://settings/certificates** in the **URL** field and press Enter. The Certificate Manager appears.

2. Select the **Authorities** tab and then click **Import**.

3. Navigate to your crt file and click **Open**.

4. Enable the **Trust this site for Identifying Web Sites** check box and then click **OK**.

5. Click **Done** and reload your page. You should now be presented with the green padlock of great justice!

Installing a Server Certificate on Mozilla Firefox

Unlike Chrome, installing the server certificate as a valid authority won't calm Firefox down — it will always throw a warning when you connect to a site secured with a self-signed certificate until you add an exception.

1. Navigate to https://s.s.s.s, where s.s.s.s is the public IP of your web server. Firefox will display a warning.

2. Click **Advanced**, then click **Add Exception**. The Add Security Exception dialog appears.

3. Ensure that **Permanently store this exception** is enabled and then click **Confirm Security Exception**.

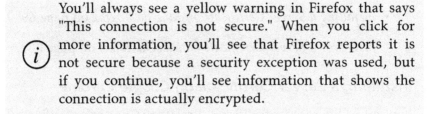

You'll always see a yellow warning in Firefox that says "This connection is not secure." When you click for more information, you'll see that Firefox reports it is not secure because a security exception was used, but if you continue, you'll see information that shows the connection is actually encrypted.

Installing a Server Certificate on Apple Safari on OSX

It's important to note how Safari deals with untrusted pages — if a certificate is deemed non-trustworthy, you'll receive a warning. However, once you dismiss the warning, you'll never see another error — you just won't see a lock. This isn't great, because you may think you're using a secure connection, the URL has "https" in it, but nothing alerts you that what you're looking at could be either mixed content or not secured. If you're on a secure site, however, you will see a little lock in the URL.

To install the root certificate in OSX:

1. Open Spotlight, and search for your certificate name. When it appears, click to open it.

2. It will import the certificate into Keychain Access and you'll be prompted for your Administrative password.

3. Enter your password when prompted. You'll see your certificate was added, and it should appear in red, as untrusted.

4. Double-click the certificate and, in the certificate's properties, change **When using this certificate** to **Always Trust**.

5. Close the properties list and provide your administrative password when prompted.

6. Close Keychain Access and reload your site in Safari.

7

Configuring Client Connections to OpenVPN Server

Now that your OpenVPN server is up and running and you have a secure place to serve configuration files, we need to create these configuration files and get them installed them on your computers and mobile devices.

In this chapter, we'll create client configuration files and install them on commonly-used clients, including Ubuntu Linux, Mac OSX, Windows 10, ChromeBook, iPhone, and Android.

OpenVPN clients require three basic components: an OpenVPN client application, an OpenVPN configuration file, and connection authentication files (the client's private key, the client's certificate, and the issuing certificate authority's certificate).

In our case, we've added an additional security step and are including a TLS authentication certificate to further encrypt the channel.

OpenVPN configuration files use the .ovpn file extension — and you can embed the certificates and key inside the file. This simplifies the connection process as you will only need to install an OpenVPN client on the device and import a single file to connect.

If you're using a Google Chromebook, you'll also need a copy of your client's keys in PKCS12 format and the configuration file

73

must be converted to a file format that Chromebook can import — but don't worry, we've got a small script that will do the heavy lifting for you!

As you get more experience, you can use any of the client samples in /usr/share/doc/openvpn-2.4.7/sample/sample-config-files on the OpenVPN server to craft ovpn connection files.

To create a client configuration file:

1. From the shell on your OpenVPN server, change into your home directory and clone this book's companion github repository:

   ```
   [ec2-user~]$ cd ~/ && git clone \
   https://github.com/diy-vpn/diy-vpn.git
   ```

2. Move into the directory and run mkcliconf.py. We'll use the default options because we've got a known setup. The script does allow you to change the locations of your server.conf and certificate store (pki directory) if you've customized your installation:

   ```
   [ec2-user~]$ cd diy-vpn/mkcliconf && \
   ssudo python mkcliconf.py
   ```

3. This should place three files in your current directory: *servername*.com.onc, *servername*.p12, and *servername*.ovpn (where *servername* is the common name of the certificate authority you created in *Installing and Configuring OpenVPN Server)* on page 35.

4. Next, copy your client.ovpn file to the /var/www/html/downloads directory that you created in *Password-protecting Your Download Directory* on page 65 and change its ownership so that the web server can display it:

   ```
   [ec2-user~]$ sudo cp host_address.* \
   /var/www/html/downloads/

   [ec2-user~]$ sudo chown -R apache:apache \
   /var/www/html/downloads
   ```

Our script writes certificate and key data within the file so that it's easy to install as a single file for mobile and desktop clients. It is also acceptable to use the following instead of the <key/>, <ca/> and <cert/> elements and then select them when configuring the connection:

```
ca /path/to/ca.crt
cert /path/to/client.crt
key /path/to/client.key
tls-auth /path/to/ta.key
```

5. Next, open https://host_address/downloads and, when prompted, log in using the username and password you set when configuring your Apache web server. Your connection files should appear — click them to download!

7.1 Installing and Running OpenVPN on Microsoft Windows 10

OpenVPN provides a free client for Windows users. You can also use Viscosity, a paid VPN app (not too pricey at $9/license and a free monthly trial) that works for macOS and Windows. We'll describe how to connect to your VPN server using the OpenVPN Connect client.

To install and run OpenVPN Connect on Microsoft Windows 10:

1. Open a web browser and download the VPN client configuration file, host_address.ovpn, from your secure web server: https://host_address/downloads/, where host_address is your web and VPN server's address.

2. While still in the browser, navigate to https://openvpn.net/index.php/open-source/downloads.html

3. Click to download the latest Windows 10 OpenVPN client (at time or writing, this is **openvpn-install-2.4.7-I607-Win10.exe**).

4. Proceed through the wizard to install OpenVPN, accepting the default options.

5. When prompted to install the Tap provider, click **Install**.

   OpenVPN should be installed as a shortcut on the Desktop and in the System Tray (likely hidden).

6. From the System Tray, click the tiny arrow to the left of your system tray and then select **Show hidden** icons. OpenVPN's icon is the tiny monitor with a lock on it.

7. Right-click on the OpenVPN icon and select **Import File**.

8. Navigate to where you downloaded your configuration file, select it, then click **Open**. The configuration will be added.

9. Right-click on the OpenVPN icon and click **VPN Details....**

10. Tap **Settings** and enable **Route all IPv4 traffic through the VPN** and **Disable IPv6**.

11. Click **Connect**. You can also click on the OpenVPN icon, and click **Connect (profile name)**.

You should now be connected! Open your browser and navigate to https://diy-vpn.com/ip or type "What's my IP" into DuckDuckGo or Google to quickly verify that your connection is going through the VPN server, and then proceed to Verifying and Troubleshooting OpenVPN Connections on page 91 for additional tests to verify that you are successfully routing traffic through the tunnel. If you encounter any issues connecting, check the log (right-click on the icon, select your connection type, then click **View Log**) for clues.

7.2 Installing and Running OpenVPN on MacOS

To configure an OpenVPN connection in macOS, we'll use an app called Tunnelblick, which is free and open source. Viscosity is also a popular option.

To connect to your VPN server using TunnelBlick:

1. First, make sure that you haven't configured DNS servers manually set or, preferably, they are the DNS servers you want to use. Tunnelblick will not overwrite your DNS settings with your VPN's settings if they're manually configured. To do this, open **System Preferences**, tap **Network**, select your network, tap **Advanced**, then open the **DNS** page. Select each DNS server and tap the - to delete it. If these are the DNS servers you want to use, keep them. This ensures that if you aren't using the VPN, you don't drop to your ISP's default DNS settings. Then, tap **OK** and **Apply** to save your changes and close preferences.

2. Download the VPN client configuration file (host_address.ovpn) from your secure web server: https://*host_address*/downloads/, where *host_address* is your web and VPN server's address.

3. Download TunnelBlick (3.7.9a is the stable version as of publication; 3.8 is available as a beta and is suitable as well) for OSX from tunnelblick.net.

4. Double-click the dbg file to run it, and then double-click the **Tunnelblick** icon when it appears. You may receive a warning about opening applications downloaded from the Internet. Click **Open** to continue.

5. When prompted, enter your administrative password and click **OK**.

6. The application is installed. When prompted, decide whether to check for updates automatically and to send

anonymous system profile (we recommend *unchecking* this box before clicking **Don't Check** or **Check Automatically**).

7. You'll then receive an option to verify that your public IP has not changed to detect leakage — this is a cool feature, but it does ping tunnelblick.net periodically. You can decide whether you want to do this after checking out their privacy policy (click **Privacy info** to view).

8. When prompted, choose whether you want TunnelBlick to place the icon next to Spotlight or not.

9. When prompted for information about configuration files, click **I have Configuration Files.**

10. Click **OK** to dismiss the **Add a Configuration** dialog.

11. Click Finder and navigate to the directory where you stored your ovpn file. Select it, and drag it over the TunnelBlick icon in the system tray. You'll see a little green circle with a white + inside it when you're in the right spot!

12. Drop the ovpn file on the icon.

13. When prompted, select whether you'd like all users of the computer or only you to connect to the VPN.

14. When prompted, enter your password and click **OK**. You should receive an installation successful message.

15. To connect to your VPN, mouse over the Tunnelblick icon and click **Connect client** (if you named your configuration file differently, you'll see a different connection name).

You should now be successfully connected! Open your browser and navigate to https://diy-vpn.com/ip or Google "What's my IP?" to verify that your connection is going through the VPN server, and then proceed to *Verifying and Troubleshooting OpenVPN Connections* on page 91 for additional tests to verify that you are successfully routing traffic through the tunnel. If you encounter any issues connecting, check the log (right-click on the icon, select your connection type, then click **View Log**).

7.3 Installing and Running OpenVPN on Ubuntu Linux

If you haven't used an OpenVPN VPN client on your computer before, you must first install a few packages to support it adding an OpenVPN connection to Network Manager.

A note for Linux clients who plan to run OpenVPN from the command line: If you're using Ubuntu, add the following lines to your .ovpn file to ensure that your DNS server entries are updated by OpenVPN:

```
script-security 2
up "/etc/openvpn/update-resolv-conf"
down "/etc/openvpn/update-resolv-conf"
```

If you're planning on running on any Linux variant from the command line, you'll also want to configure the client to not run as root after it starts (for CentOS/Red Hat-based OS variants, change nogroup to nobody):

```
user nobody
group nogroup # use nobody for non-Debian-based systems
```

You don't need to do this if you're installing the configuration using Network Manager. In testing with Ubuntu 16.04, Network Manager adds and deletes DNS entries appropriately — unless absolutely necessary, you should use Network Manager to handle your VPN connection, both for this reason and because it's easier to enable/disable/visually see your connection status at a glance. Also, do not add these lines to Windows client configuration files — it will cause them to break.

To configure a client connection on Ubuntu Linux:

1. Download the VPN client configuration file, `host_address.ovpn` from your secure web server: https:// *host_address*/downloads/, where *host_address* is your web and VPN server's address.

2. Run the following command to install OpenVPN support on your operating system (if you already have OpenVPN support installed, jump to step 4):

```
[ec2-user~]$ sudo apt-get install openvpn \
network-manager-openvpn network-manager-openvpn-gnome
```

 If you receive an error that package manager can't find it (this can happen if you're using a Live CD or minimal install), run `sudo nano /etc/apt/sources.list`, uncomment the final line that lists the source for the the universe repository, then run `sudo apt-get update`.

3. Restart Network Manager:

```
[ec2-user~]$ sudo systemctl restart network-manager
```

4. Right-click on your network connection icon in the system tray and click **Edit Connections**.

5. Click **Add**. The Choose a Connection Type dialog appears.

6. Select **Import a saved VPN Configuration** from the very bottom of the list and click **Create....** When prompted, navigate to the location where you saved the configuration, then click **Open**. Click **Save**. Close Network Connections.

7. Click on your wifi connection indicator in the system tray, select **VPN Connections**, then select the configuration you just imported.

You should now be successfully connected! Open your browser and navigate to `https://diy-vpn.com/ip` or just type "What's my IP" into Google. for quick confirmation that your connection is going through the VPN server, and then proceed to *Verifying and Troubleshooting OpenVPN Connections* on page 91 for additional tests to verify hat you are successfully routing traffic through the tunnel. If you encounter any problems connecting, check `/var/log/syslog` for clues.

 Sometimes, if you're doing a lot of VPN testing and changing network status a lot, Ubuntu's network will get into a state where it can't even connect to wifi or the UI won't show your VPN connections. To recover from this condition without rebooting, restart Network Manager from the command line: sudo systemctl restart network-manager.

7.4   Installing and Running OpenVPN on iPhones

Installing and running OpenVPN on iPhones requires two items: The OpenVPN Connect app and your ovpn file.

1. Download and install the **OpenVPN Connect** client app from the Apple App Store.

2. Open Safari and navigate to https://*host_address*/ downloads/, where *host_address* is your web and VPN server's address. Click to download the your `host_address.ovpn` file. The file will download and display **Open in "OpenVPN"** at the top or bottom of the page (depending on your version).

3. Click **Open in "OpenVPN."** The OpenVPN app launches, displaying a **New Profiles Are Available** message.

4. Click the green circle with the check box beneath the profile to install it.

5. Next, toggle the connection to enable it.

6. When prompted to allow OpenVPN to enable VPN connection, tap **Yes**. You can now enable and disable the VPN from the iPhone Settings app.

You should now be successfully connected! Open your browser and navigate to https://diy-vpn.com/ip or Google "What's my IP?" to quickly verify that your connection is going through the VPN server, and then proceed to *Verifying and Troubleshooting OpenVPN Connections* on page 91 for additional tests to verify that you are successfully routing traffic through the tunnel. If you encounter any issues connecting, check the log (expand the **Connected/Disconnected** list item) for clues.

> If you are successfully connected and do *not* see the VPN IP as your IP address, are you running iOS 9? If so, make sure you configured push "redirect-gateway ipv6" in your server.conf as discussed in the *Installing and Configuring OpenVPN Server* on page 35. There's a bug on iOS 9 where, if ipv6 tunneling routes are pushed down by the OpenVPN server, ipv4 traffic is routed outside the VPN. This can be resolved using the redirect-gateway setting for IPv6 on the server side.

7.5 Installing and Running OpenVPN on Android Phones

Installing and running OpenVPN on Android requires two items: The OpenVPN Connect app and your ovpn file.

To install the OpenVPN client on an Android device:

1. Download the OpenVPN Connect app from Google Play.

2. Open your browser and navigate to https://*host_address*/ downloads/, where *host_address* is your web and VPN server's address.

3. Download the `host_address.ovpn` file, then click on it to launch OpenVPN.

4. Click **Accept** to accept the profile.

5. Click **Connect** to connect.

You should now be successfully connected! Open your browser and navigate to https://diy-vpn.com/ip or Google "What's my IP?" to quickly verify that your connection is traversing the VPN server, and then proceed to *Verifying and Troubleshooting OpenVPN Connections* on page 91 for additional tests to verify that you are successfully routing traffic through the tunnel. If you encounter any issues connecting, check the log for clues.

7.6   Installing and Running OpenVPN on ChromeBook

ChromeOS on the Chromebook doesn't have the capability to import OpenVPN configuration files and is missing the options you'd need to configure the connection manually using their network manager.

This leaves you with three options: enable "developer mode" and run `openvpn` from the `crosh` shell (kind of defeats the purpose of a Chromebook and is inconvenient if you aren't already using developer mode), install the OpenVPN Connect app for Android on the Chromebook (it works, but it's a little awkward to enable and disable)– or convert the ovpn file to ONC (Open Network Configuration) format so that Google can understand it natively so that you can enable and disable it from the system tray.

Luckily, we've already generated our ONC file and there's a hidden place in ChromeOS to import it.

To connect to your VPN server using Chromebook:

1. On your Chromebook, open Chrome and download *host_address*.onc and *host_address*.p12 from your secure web server: https://*host_address*/downloads/, where

host_address is your web and VPN server location. Make a note of where you saved the files (the default Downloads directory is fine, just delete them afterwards).

2. In Chrome, navigate to **chrome://settings/certificates**.

3. Click **Import & Bind to Device** and, when prompted, select *host_address*.p12. When prompted again, enter the password chrome and press Enter. This password is set inside the mkcliconf.py generator script we ran to generate configuration files; you can change it in the script and re-run if you like.

4. After importing the p12 file, navigate to **chrome://net-internals** and select **ChromeOS** from the bottom of the left-side menu.

5. Click **Import ONC**, navigate to your downloaded servername.onc file, then click **Import**. After you've done this, the page will still display the message "No file chosen," but fear not! That's just a bug in the interface. Tap your wifi network icon in the system tray, tap **VPN Connection**, and it should show up there, ready to connect.

6. From the wifi icon > **VPN** menu (you may have to expand the menu using ^ to display it), select your server name to **Connect**. You'll be prompted for a password.

   If you didn't configure username/password authentication on the server, you can put anything you like here, but make sure it's something (that's not an actual password!) — the server doesn't care if it doesn't need it, but ChromeOS's network management user interface won't let you move forward without a value — any value — in the username and password fields.

   Note that if you have multiple VPN connections set up this way, the network manager may assign the wrong certificate to your VPN connection. This is easily fixed via the VPN configuration page, just scroll down to certificate and change it to the certificate that matches the ONC file.

You should now be successfully connected! Open your browser and navigate to https://diy-vpn.com/ip or Google "What's my IP?" to quickly verify that your connection is going through the VPN server, and then proceed to *Verifying and Troubleshooting OpenVPN Connections* on page 91 for additional tests to verify that you are successfully routing traffic through the tunnel.

8

Using Your VPN Server to Block Ads

One neat thing about running your own VPN server is that you can use it to block ads. This is especially useful for mobile devices, as ad blocker usage and installation on mobile devices is not quite as easy as installing an ad blocker on your desktop browser.

To block ads at the VPN server, we'll first redirect all requests to known ad servers to the local system using the system's hosts file, located at /etc/hosts. Luckily for us, a helpful developer, Steven Black, periodically compiles a hosts file that contains a comprehensive list of ad networks to block from a variety of sources. It's updated often and we can use this to replace our own hosts file.

We'll then install Dnsmasq on the system, allowing it to act as a DNS server for any connected VPN clients.

Then, we'll update our VPN server configuration to push a new DNS configuration down that tells clients to use the VPN server as its DNS server.

Note that we did this automatically in *Launching a VPN and Web Server in Five Minutes* on page 11 with the following lines, as well as including push "dhcp-option DNS 10.8.0.1" added to the server.conf:

```
cd /home/ec2-user && wget \
https://raw.githubusercontent.com/\StevenBlack/hosts/master/hosts
sudo mv -f /home/ec2-user/hosts /etc/hosts
sudo yum -y install dnsmasq
sudo systemctl start dnsmasq
sudo systemctl enable dnsmasq
```

Are there drawbacks to this approach? Yes. Blocking ads can break some sites. If you need to unblock a site, it's not quite so easy as disabling your ad blocker; you'll need to get to the server, comment out the site you want to access, then re-try. Alternatively, you could just disconnect from your VPN, get to where you need to get, then re-connect when you're done.

1. Log into your VPN server and download the comprehensive list of hosts to block:

   ```
   [ec2-user~]$ wget https://raw.githubusercontent.com/\
   StevenBlack/hosts/master/hosts
   ```

2. Copy the hosts file over your existing hosts file:

   ```
   [ec2-user~]$ sudo mv -f hosts /etc/hosts
   ```

3. Install Dnsmasq, start it, and add it to system startup:

   ```
   [ec2-user~]$ sudo yum -y install dnsmasq
   [ec2-user~]$ sudo systemctl start dnsmasq
   [ec2-user~]$ sudo systemctl enable dnsmasq
   ```

4. Stop OpenVPN:

   ```
   [ec2-user~]$ systemctl stop openvpn
   ```

5. Add the following line to /etc/openvpn/server.conf:

```
push "dhcp-option DNS 10.8.0.1"
```

6. Restart OpenVPN:

```
[ec2-user~]$ sudo systemctl start openvpn
```

7. Open the firewall so that clients can connect to the Dnsmasq service:

```
[ec2-user~]$ sudo firewall-cmd -zone=public -add-service dns \
  --permanent
[ec2-user~]$ sudo firewall-cmd --reload
```

8. Disconnect your clients from your VPN server and reconnect.

> ⓘ To ensure that you're always getting the latest ad servers, you can configure a scheduled task (cron job) to periodically and automatically update the hosts file.

9. Create a file at /home/ec2-user/hosts.sh with the following commands:

```
cd /home/ec2-user && wget https://raw.githubusercontent.com/\
StevenBlack/hosts/master/hosts

sudo mv -f /home/ec2-user/hosts /etc/hosts
```

10. Type the following to open the Linux scheduler, cron's schedule:

```
[ec2-user~]$ crontab -e
```

11. Paste the following, where 5 indicates that the script should be run at 5:30AM UTC every day (the first entry is minute, then hour, then day, then week, then month, followed by the command to be run. Because we opened crontab using the ec2-user, it's assumed that the ec2-user runs the task. In a later section, we'll edit the daily crontab file, and in that case will specify which user runs the task):

```
30 5 * * * sh /home/ec2-user/hosts.sh
```

12. Save and close the file.

You can verify that it works by running `ls -la /etc/hosts` periodically to see that the file has a newer timestamp.

You can also edit crontab to run more often to see it in action, then change it to a lower frequency setting. For example, you could use `*/2 * * * * sh /home/ec2-user/hosts.sh` to run the script every two minutes just to make sure everything works.

Run `watch ls -la /home/ec2-user/hosts.sh` to watch the file time update in real-time!

9

Verifying and Troubleshooting OpenVPN Connections

You should now be connected to the Internet using your secure and personal VPN. Now's a good time to verify that everything is working correctly.

9.1 Ensure All Traffic is Using the VPN Tunnel

You can use external sites to verify that your connections aren't leaking. A quick way to do this is to visit https://ipleak.net, which can show you which IP you're connecting through, which DNS servers you're using, whether you're using IPv6, and other useful privacy-related data points. You should see your VPN's IP address here and the DNS servers associated with the DNS provider you set in your server configuration. You shouldn't see any DNS servers used by your ISP.

Because our setup does not support forwarding IPv6 traffic, you'll see an IPv6 test not reachable alert.

https://ipv6leak.net provides a quick leak test for IPv6, and https://dnsleak.net has a test for DNS leaks.

These sites are a great start and sanity check to make sure everything's working as it should — but you may also want to test your connection directly. (Also note that, while very useful, many leak-checking sites exist to sell you their own VPN service!)

Hands-on Connection Testing

Let's take a real-world example. Say you want to ensure that secure email traffic from your phone is successfully tunneling through your VPN. Now, you know your web traffic through Safari is fine because when you visit a web site, it shows your IP as your VPN server's IP. But how do you test your email traffic? Here are two quick ways to validate specific traffic flows, one of which you can use to validate third party VPNs that you don't have access to.

Testing email throughput from the VPN server (the fun way):

1. Install ngrep (network grep) on your VPN server:

```
[ec2-user~]$ wget https://dl.fedoraproject.org/pub/\
epel/epel-release-latest-7.noarch.rpm

[ec2-user~]$ sudo rpm -ivh \
epel-release-latest-7.noarch.rpm

[ec2-user~]$ sudo yum -y install ngrep
```

   What this does is enable the Extra Packages for Enterprise Linux (or EPEL) repository so that you can install software packages from the Fedora Community Project that are not included in Amazon's default distribution.

2. Run ngrep with a filter that looks for your secure mail traffic (imaps, which runs on port 993):

```
[ec2-user~]$ sudo ngrep -q port 993
```

   In this command, we run ngrep (we must sudo to root to access the network interface) with -q, which stands for quiet mode (it excludes hashes that are sent to show traffic received that doesn't match the filter we set), and we set our filter to look for traffic on port 993, the secure mail (imaps) port.

3. On your phone, open up your Mail app while watching your ngrep command. You should see some gobbledy-gook (aka encrypted traffic) that looks a bit like:

```
T 209.85.232.109:993 -> 172.30.2.120:64818 [AP]
...%.........0{..[@~.L..3....\_...s.S....F.
```

So here, we see that our VPN client running on 172.30.2.120 received a packet from 209.85.232.109 on port 993. If we install the whois program (yum -y install jwhois), we can run whois 209.85.232.109 and verify that yes, that's Gmail — mail traffic *is* being routed through the tunnel.

4. To exit ngrep, press CTRL-C. There are other options and filters you can use with ngrep. To see a list of options and examples, type ngrep -h from the command line.

If you installed OSSEC as described in *Installing OSSEC to Monitor for Network Intrusions* on page 99 (don't worry if you haven't yet, it's in the next chapter!), you may have received a barrage of email alerts — for the installation of new packages and new users for those packages, and alerts for each time you bind to the interface. You can disable these alerts if you like, or keep them so that you see when actions like this occur.

A practical way to verify your email traffic *and* a way to verify that third party VPN providers work:

1. Send an email to yourself while attached to the VPN.

2. After it's sent, open it up and View Original — you'll see headers that look like:

```
Return-Path: <me@myemailaddress.com>
Received: from [10.8.0.6] (ec2-52-6-20-195.compute-1.amazonaws.
com. [52.6.20.195])
by smtp.gmail.com with ESMTPSA id a21sm9688417qkj.54.2017.04.03.
07.33.20
for <me@myemailaddress.com>
(version=TLS1_2 cipher=ECDHE-RSA-AES128-GCM-SHA256 bits=128/128);
Mon, 03 Apr 2017 07:33:20 -0700 (PDT)
```

```
From: Myself! <me@myemailaddress.com>
Content-Type: text/plain; charset=us-ascii
Content-Transfer-Encoding: 7bit
Mime-Version: 1.0 (1.0)
Date: Mon, 3 Apr 2017 10:33:18 -0400
Subject: test
Message-Id: <21037938-D531-460A-806D-48E6FBFC9483@gmail.com>
To: "Myself!" <me@myemailaddress.com>
X-Mailer: iPhone Mail (13F69)
```

Do you see your ISP's IP in there? No? Success!

9.2   Troubleshooting OpenVPN Server

Encounter issues during your deployment? Here's a list to help you through it.

OpenVPN is logging a "Socket bind failed" message

OpenVPN looks like it's started up, you go to connect, nothing happens...check /var/log/messages and horrors! A Cannot bind to socket message. But if you run ps -e |grep openvpn to return and search a process list to see if it's running, it's not...and if you run lsof -i |grep 1194 (where 1194 is the port number you're using) to see if anything's somehow already bound to the OpenVPN port, nothing's bound...so what's up?

Check /etc/openvpn/ for other .conf files. What happens is OpenVPN sees a .conf file and tries to load it — if it sees two conf files, even is one is server.conf and the other is my_backup.conf, OpenVPN is going to try to spin up both of them (this is why the startup script prints OK when it starts up — because it doesn't check for this multi-configuration situation).

So, if you *must* edit files directly in /etc/openvpn, save that backup as my_backup.conf.*bak.*

I can connect, but DNS doesn't work on my client

Make sure IP forwarding "stuck" and that net.ipv4.ip_forward = 1. You can run sysctl -a |grep net.ipv4.ip_forward to verify.

Make sure that your OpenVPN server is pushing down DNS servers: the `server.conf` should have `push "dhcp-option DNS` entries for each server you want used (if you're running Dnsmasq to block ads, don't forget 10.8.0.1!).

Make sure only one OpenVPN process is running on the server:

```
ps -efwww |grep openvpn
```

I configured Dnsmasq to block ads, but ad servers I know are in my hosts file aren't blocked

Check to make sure that your OpenVPN `server.conf` file has `push "dhcp-option DNS 10.8.0.1"` included and OpenVPN has been stopped and started.

Also make sure you've opened the firewall for DNS:

```
sudo firewall-cmd --zone=public --add-service dns --permanent
&& sudo firewall-cmd --reload.
```

Only one user can connect at a time

Ensure that `duplicate-cn` is uncommented in your `/etc/openvpn/ server.conf` file on the server.

I changed my protocol and/or port in my server.conf and client.ovpn, and even though they match, the client can't connect

Check three things:

- Did you update your AWS Security Group to allow external access to the new port and protocol?

- Make sure openvpn shows up in allowed services on the firewall: `sudo firewall-cmd --list-all`

- Any chance you missed changing the ipv6 protocol? You should have two items in your server config for each to avoid ipv6 leaks: `proto tcp` and `proto tcp6`. For udp, `proto udp` and `proto udp6`.

- Did you restart OpenVPN on the server after making a change? (`sudo systemctl restart openvpn`)

I can't log into my other ec2 instances when connected to the VPN

This can happen if the instance you're trying to connect to doesn't have a Security Group rule to allow the VPN's *public* IP address to access it. Even if you add the two hosts to the same Security Group and set a rule for your servers to address each other directly, the rule is configured for *internal* Amazon IPs, not public. To fix this, on the AWS Management Console, navigate to **EC2 > Security Groups**, then select the your security group used by the server you want to access and ensure that your VPN's public IP address is added for the ports and protocols you'd like to use.

When I try to install an ovpn file in Linux, I see a message saying the import plugin isn't available, but Network Manager with VPN support is definitely installed

Check `/var/log/syslog` and you might see:

```
Message: vpn: (vpnc,/usr/lib/NetworkManager/VPN/nm-vpnc-
service.name) file "/usr/lib/x86_64-linux-gnu/NetworkManager/
libnm-vpn-plugin-vpnc.so" not found. Did you install the
client package?"
```

Not a helpful error message and it may get you spinning! Try running `openvpn --config your_file_name.conf` from the command line, that will provide you with a much more useful error: you've probably got a syntax error you can quickly fix in the `.ovpn` file.

One other tip for Linux, especially Network Manager: Network Manager sometimes can get itself into a useless state that requires you to restart it: `sudo service NetworkManager restart` or `sudo systemctl restart NetworkManager`, depending on your Linux distribution.

My client can't connect, even though other clients of the same type can

Double-check that the time on your client is set correctly.

10

Installing OSSEC to Monitor for Network Intrusions

OSSEC is an open source intrusion detection system that monitors your application log files for suspicious activity and periodically checks your file system for changes. When you install it, you can configure it to send email alerts alerts when suspicious activity or system changes occur. It's very configurable and you can task it with monitoring log files for anything you like. It can even run specific commands and check the output.

OSSEC comes with a large default ruleset that encompasses a wide range of network devices and applications, including alerts for VPN authentication errors and network scans or attacks against your web server.

Plus, a fun bonus for the curious and the paranoid: If Amazon pushes an update and you install it, OSSEC will log every system change. (If you're truly paranoid, you may not want all system version changes sent over email — email alerts can be easily disabled.)

If you plan to open your VPN server to public access (and even if you don't), it's important that you have some sort of tripwire or monitoring system to alert you to suspicious activity.

10.1 Installing and Configuring OSSEC

To install and start OSSEC:

1. On your server, install the C code compiler, gcc, as we'll be building OSSEC from its source code (note that gcc may already be installed, but you'll find out one way or another after running the following command):

   ```
   [ec2-user@ ~]$ sudo yum -y install gcc
   ```

2. Use git to clone the OSSEC repository and check out the OSSEC repository for version 3.3 (you should already have git installed for previous operations in this guide, but if not you can install it via sudo yum -y install git). We'll be cloning the repository and checking out version 3.3.0:

   ```
   [ec2-user@ ~]$ git clone https://github.com/ossec/\
   ossec-hids.git -single-branch 3.3.0
   ```

3. This version needs a few extras before the install will run. First, we'll download and copy the PCRE (Perl-compatible Regular Expression) libraries that OSSEC uses to pattern match to the place the OSSEC installer will look for them:

   ```
   [ec2-user~]$ wget \
   https://ftp.pcre.org/pub/pcre/pcre2-10.32.tar.gz

   [ec2-user~]$ tar -xzvf pcre2-10.32.tar.gz \
   -C 3.3.0/src/external/
   ```

4. Next, we'll install the libevent C library:

   ```
   [ec2-user~]$ sudo yum -y install libevent-devel
   ```

5. Start the installation:

   ```
   [ec2-user~]$ cd 3.3.0 && sudo sh install.sh
   ```

6. Choose a language or accept the default (English) and press Enter.

7. Press Enter when prompted to start the installation.

8. When prompted to select the type of installation, enter local.

9. Press Enter to select the default installation location (/var/ossec).

10. If you'd like to receive email notifications for high impact events, press Enter to select [y].

11. Then, when prompted, enter the email address you'd like to use. OSSEC will attempt to determine the mail server to use to send your email. Gmail may not work, but the system has a local sendmail instance — you can change this to 127.0.0.1 later in /var/ossec/etc/ossec.conf if you run into issues with Gmail's server and that should do the trick.

 While out-of-scope for this particular guide, if you're interested in setting up your own quickie serverless mail server on EC2 using Amazon SES, check out the tutorial at https://diy-vpn.com/post/2017-05-10-amazon-ses-and-gmail/.

12. Enter y to continue. If you do not want to configure email alerts, type n and press Enter.

13. Next, you'll be asked if you want to install the integrity daemon. This will do a daily scan of binaries and files that aren't expected to change, and will alert you to anything that changes. This can be good for verifying that you have not had binaries changed on the system without your knowledge (note that you'll get alerts when you update your system). Press Enter to accept and continue.

14. You'll be asked whether you want to run the rootkit detection engine. Press Enter to accept and continue.

15. Next, you'll be asked if you want to enable active response and firewall drop rules. This feature allows OSSEC to set firewall rules to block an IP address if it detects abuse — repeated scanning or repeated failed log in attempts. Note that you can also add your own rules once OSSEC is installed.

16. OSSEC next detects your internal network and adds it to a list of IP addresses that it will never block. Type y here and add your own IP address to ensure that you aren't ever locked out! You can add multiple addresses, separated by spaces, and can use subnet masks (10.10.10.0/24, for example) to the list of never-to-be-blocked hosts.

17. Press Enter to complete configuration and begin the installation.

18. After OSSEC has completed installation, press Enter and start OSSEC:

```
[ec2-user~]$ sudo /var/ossec/bin/ossec-control start
```

OSSEC will start. Because OpenVPN logs directly to /var/log/messages, which OSSEC monitors, you'll almost immediately start to receive a few alerts. In addition to the email alerts it set up, OSSEC will log rule violations to /var/ossec/logs/ossec.log.

Because it runs default searches for errors and has a set of VPN rules installed, you'll get notifications for connection errors and other types of errors your VPN server reports, in addition to other potential security issues in other system components, including your web server.

10.2   Customizing OSSEC Alerting

Any rule configured with a priority higher than 7 (where 1 is the highest priority) will trigger an email alert and will write an alert to the log file, and violations lower than 7 are just written to log files.   You can change this in the <email_alert_level> element inside ossec.conf.   You can also disable email alerts by changing the <email_notifications> value from yes to no.

We'll walk through an example you might want to implement: Updating OpenVPN's configuration to log to its own file and then adding that OpenVPN log file to OSSEC's list of monitored files.

To add new files for monitoring:

1. Update your /etc/openvpn/server.conf file to log to its own file by uncommenting log (log by itself will overwrite the log on startup, deleting the previous one. log-append will append to the current log) and then restart OpenVPN (sudo systemctl stop openvpn && sudo systemctl start openvpn — note that there is a restart option, but because we're running as nobody instead of root, restart fails. There's a way around this using OpenVPN's root-down plugin, but stop and start does the trick just as easily for us!).

2. Add openvpn.log to the list of files to modify inside your OSSEC configuration:

   ```
   [ec2-user~]$ sudo nano /var/ossec/etc/ossec.conf
   ```

3. Locate   the   <!-- Files to monitor (localfiles) --> comment and place a stub like the following:

   ```
   <!-- Files to monitor (localfiles) -->
   <localfile>
     <log_format>syslog</log_format>
     <location>/etc/openvpn/openvpn.log</location>
   </localfile>
   ```

103

There are different format types you can choose from: syslog, snort-full, snort-fast, squid, iis, eventlog (for Windows event logs), mysql_log, postgresql_log, nmapg or apache. This is neat because it can understand Apache access and error logs right out of the box, as well as Squid logs (if you choose at some point to add Squid, a caching web proxy, to your deployment).

4. Next, we'll want to remove /etc/openvpn/openvpn.log and /etc/openvpn/openvpn-status.log from syscheck monitoring: syscheck alerts you when files on the system change and because we know these files will change often, we don't want OSSEC to alert us every time. To do that, locate <syscheck>, and beneath it, add an entry for both files:

```
<syscheck>
<!-- Frequency that syscheck is executed - default to every
22 hours->
<frequency>79200</frequency>

<!-- Directories to check (perform all possible
verifications) -->
<directories check_all="yes">/etc,/usr/bin,/usr/sbin</directories>
<directories check_all="yes">/bin,/sbin,/boot</directories>

<!-- Files/directories to ignore -->
<ignore>/etc/openvpn/openvpn.log</ignore>
<ignore>/etc/openvpn/openvpn-status.log</ignore>
<ignore>/etc/mtab</ignore>
<ignore>/etc/mnttab</ignore>
<ignore>/etc/hosts.deny</ignore>
```

5. Save and close the file and restart OSSEC:

```
[ec2-user~]$ sudo /var/ossec/bin/ossec-control restart
```

That should stop the alerts we were receiving about a rule that had been firing about that we don't care about: Rule 552, which triggers when a file changes.

10.3 Creating Custom Rules for OSSEC

After using OSSEC for awhile, and if you're feeling adventurous, you may decide you want to create custom rules to capture specific actions that the default rule set may not capture.

Because the rule set provided by OSSEC is so extensive, you may never need to create a custom rule, but it's good to have the information just in case!

In this demonstration, we'll create a rule that sends an alert for connection errors that may indicate that either our clients are having connection issues or unauthorized users are attempting to use our VPN.

Note that if you're using the default alerting configuration, with OpenVPN logging to the system's default log (`/var/log/syslog`), you should already receive these alerts as OSSEC will trigger on the word "ERROR" in the default log, but as it may be useful for you to know how to create your own alerts for error conditions specific to your VPN (and to quiet down any alerts you may not find useful), we're going to create specific rules for OpenVPN.

Configure OpenVPN to Log to its Own File

First, let's make sure that OpenVPN is logging where we want it to. In its default configuration, OpenVPN logs to the system's log. But to keep things discrete and ensure that OpenVPN's logs aren't intermingled in system logs, we'll modify OpenVPN's logging configuration.

1. Open up `/etc/openvpn/server.conf` in your favorite text editor:

   ```
   [ec2-user~]$ sudo nano /etc/openvpn/server.conf
   ```

2. If you used the sample file, you'll see the following line:

   ```
   # log /var/log/openvpn.log
   ```

105

3. Remove the # sign and change `log` to `log-append`. Your log line should look like:

```
log-append /var/log/openvpn.log
```

The `append` part is important for our testing. We originally configured our system *not* to append to a log, which clears the log on restart. This is useful for security and privacy.

For our current use case, we want to create logs to use for rule construction, so removing those logs on restart is suboptimal. So let's change this to append while we construct our rules, then we can always change it back to a non-appending log after we've finished crafting and testing our OSSEC rules.

4. Save and close the file.

5. Restart OpenVPN:

```
[ec2-user~]$ sudo systemctl stop openvpn
[ec2-user~]$ sudo systemctl start openvpn
```

6. Verify that the log file exists and has recently been modified:

```
[ec2-user~]$ sudo ls -lah /var/log/openvpn.log
```

Populate Your Log File with "Good" and "Bad" Data

Now, we'll want to populate our log file with "good" and "bad" data to better understand what we're looking for. Connect and disconnect to your VPN a few times to get "good" data, and then, set up some failure conditions so that you know what bad connections look like.

1. Generate some connection errors:

   - Enable PAM password authentication on the server, then attempt to connect with no login information (or wrong information). You can enable password authentication by adding:

     ```
     plugin /usr/lib64/openvpn/plugins/openvpn-plugin-\
     auth-pam.so login
     ```

     to your server.conf file. Restart OpenVPN (see *Require User Names and Passwords in Addition to Certificates in OpenVPN* on page 121 for step-by-step instructions if you want to use this in your configuration more permanently) and try to connect. (Once you've failed a time or two, update your configuration and restart OpenVPN.)

   - Add a new network configuration on your VPN client with incorrect or missing keys and attempt to connect.

2. Verify that you've got the data you want in your openvpn.log file by running grep to search for the word "error" (using -i to indicate that we want any lowercase or uppercase combination):

   ```
   [ec2-user@~ ]$ sudo grep -i error /var/log/openvpn.log
   ```

If you don't see any results here (or not as many errors as you believe you generated), make sure that you used log-append in your server.conf and restarted OpenVPN as described in the previous section. If `log-append` isn't used, the logs are blown away each time OpenVPN restarts.

Add the log files you want to monitor to ossec.conf

Now we've got to tell OSSEC to start monitoring our OpenVPN log.

1. Open up `/var/ossec/etc/ossec.conf` and, near the end of the file (before `</ossec_config>`), add the following:

   ```
   <localfile>
     <log_format>syslog</log_format>
     <location>/var/log/openvpn.log</location>
   </localfile>
   ```

   We use syslog here as it's recommended for log files that have one entry per line. Available values for `log_format` are `syslog`, `snort-full`, `snort-fast`, `squid`, `iis`, `eventlog` (for Windows event logs), `mysql_log`, `postgresql_log`, `nmapg`, or `apache`.

2. Restart OSSEC:

   ```
   [ec2-user@~ ]$ sudo /var/ossec/bin/ossec-control restart
   ```

> (i) If you ever find yourself monitoring log files that contain changeable dates in their filenames, OSSEC understands `strftime` (see http://www.openbsd.org/cgi-bin/man.cgi?query=strftime for more information) variables. So, for example, if your log file was `/var/log/httpd/access.log.2019-07-10`, you can set location to `<location>/var/log/httpd/access.log.%Y-%m-%d</location>`.
>
> You can render a `strftime` variable at the command line to verify it quickly. Just type `date +%X` at the command line, where X is the strftime variable. `date +%Y-%m-%d` gives us the string we need for our access logs, `date +%s` gives us Epoch time UTC.

Create a custom decoder

OSSEC uses decoders to parse log files. After it finds the proper decoder for a log, it will parse out fields defined in /var/ossec/etc/decoder.xml, then compare these values to values in rule files — and will trigger an alert when values in the deciphered log file match values specified in rule files. These values can also be passed to active response commands, which we enabled when we installed OSSEC.

In this example, we want to trigger an alert on log lines that look like our OpenVPN connection errors:

```
Tue Jul  2 18:43:39 2019 192.168.0.15:58906 TLS Error: Auth Username/
Password was not provided by peer
Tue Jul  2 18:45:52 2019 TLS Error: cannot locate HMAC in  incoming
packet from [AF_INET6]::ffff:192.168.0.15:39859
```

The first error line is from an attempted connection without a username or password and the second was due to a missing TLS Auth certificate in the OpenVPN configuration file we used to connect.

Note that our TLS errors do not show up in the same spot, and they also don't have any real identifying information in the beginning since they're logged to their own file — they just show a date format. This will make our rule creation a little trickier.

Open up a new file called /var/ossec/etc/local_decoder.xml. You *could* use decoder.xml, which already exists, but using local_decoder.xml will ensure that your custom decoders aren't overwritten when you upgrade OSSEC.

First, we want to create decoders that will match our log entries. We'll use the date and first few characters to match the logs using a *regular expression*, or *regex*, which is a sequence of characters that can be used to search for specific patterns. You may already be familiar with using an asterisk to search for anything that matches, for example, *.pdf to list a group of PDFs. In this case, you're using a regex!

Note that OSSEC has its own sort of interpretation of regular expressions, so if you happen to be a regex wizard, don't get too fancy. For example, using \d{4} type regex syntax to search for four digits and \w{3} for three letters won't work with OSSEC — think simpler and you'll have more success: you have to use \d\d\d\d and \w\w\w instead.

In the following decoder, we'll use the log files' date format and the beginning of the lines to "pre-match" the message.

This looks really complicated, but it's actually pretty simple:

- \w stands for any letter

- \d stands for any number

- \s for a space

- + means there must be at least one of the character type, but can be more

- Any literal string matches the exact letters/numbers/characters (for example, we'll use a : between digits because that's how the time is displayed)

- ^ tells OSSEC to look at the beginning of a line

- $ signifies the end of a line

Our log lines always start with a date and time in the format of Ddd Mmm dd hh:mm:ss YYYY (Mon Jan 1 00:00:00 2019), so we'll use the following decoder for our first log line that appeared during a username/password authentication failure (Tue Jul 2 18:43:39 2019 192.168.0.15:58906 TLS Error: Auth Username/Password was not provided by peer).

```
<decoder name="openvpn-bad-pass">
<prematch>^\w\w\w\s\w\w\w\s+\d+\s\d\d(:)\d\d(:)\d\d\s\d\d\d\d
</prematch>
 <regex offset="after_prematch">(\d+.\d+.\d+.\d+):\d+ TLS Error: Auth
 Username/Password was not provided by peer</regex>
 <order>srcip</order>
</decoder>
```

In the "prematch" section, we look for a pattern where the beginning of the line (^) contains three letters and a space (Tue), three more letters (Jul), one or more spaces and one or more numbers (to accommodate a one or two digit date, since it's July 2, there are two spaces before the date; but July 10th through 31st will have only one), a set of three two-digit numbers separated with colons (the time!), and the four digit year and spaces around it. (Note that this should all be on a single line inside the `local_decoder` file; we've separated it into two while typesetting this book, but there should be no space between either of the `<prematch>` tags and the inner regular expression.)

So this will match the beginning of our log line. After this, the IP address we need (one or more digits, separated by periods) appears in the log line followed by the error text.

We want to extract this source IP to use in blocking and reporting rules, so we tell OSSEC to extract it by placing the rest of what we want to match inside a `regex` element and telling OSSEC that we want to look for matches after we match the `prematch` text.

To extract the IP, we include the data we want to extract within parentheses (`\d+.\d+.\d+.\d+`), and then tell OSSEC to stuff this value into a source IP variable by following up the regex with an `order` element with the value `srcip`.

This `srcip` is the IP we may want to use later in our OSSEC rules. For example, we may want to create a rule that ignores errors from specific IP addresses (our own, when testing, for example — we don't want OSSEC to block us from our own server!) or an active response rule to block systems that are trying to connect but shouldn't be.

We'll do the same thing for the other error we want to block on, a user connecting with a bad certificate:

```
Tue Jul  2 18:45:52 2019 TLS Error: cannot locate HMAC in incoming
 packet from [AF_INET6]::ffff:192.168.0.15:39859
```

```
<decoder name="openvpn-bad-cert">
<prematch>^\w\w\w\s\w\w\w\s+\d+\s\d\d(:)\d\d(:)\d\d\s\d\d\d\d TLS
 Error:</prematch>
<regex offset="after_prematch">cannot locate HMAC in incoming packet
from [AF_INET6]::ffff:(\d+.\d+.\d+.\d+):</regex>
<order>srcip</order>
</decoder>
```

You can pull multiple strings if you like, using more
parentheses and adding entries inside <order> to match. A good
rule of thumb is to decode any data that you want to match
inside a rule as well as any data you might need to initiate an
active response. In that case, you'd separate each item in the
order field with a comma. OSSEC allows you to use the
following options in the order field: srcuser, dstuser, user, srcip,
dstip, srcport, dstport, protocol, id, url, action, status, and
extra_data.

As an example, you could put parentheses around the error
message, and add extra_data to order like the following to
extract the error message as well as the source IP:

```
<regex offset="after_prematch">(cannot locate HMAC in incoming packet)
from [AF_INET6]::ffff:(\d+.\d+.\d+.\d+):</regex>
<order>extra_data,srcip</order>
```

Let's take a break here, and see if our decoders work. Save and
exit   local_decoder.xml,   then   run   sudo
/var/ossec/bin/ossec-logtest.

When it opens, paste one of your log lines:

```
[ec2-user@ ~]$ sudo /var/ossec/bin/ossec-logtest
2019/07/02 20:44:27 ossec-testrule: INFO: Reading local decoder file.
2019/07/02 20:44:27 ossec-testrule: INFO: Started (pid: 19904).
ossec-testrule: Type one log per line.

Tue Jul  2 18:43:39 2019 192.168.0.15:58906 TLS Error: Auth Username/
Password was not provided by peer

**Phase 1: Completed pre-decoding.
        full event: 'Tue Jul  2 18:43:39 2019 192.168.0.15:58906 TLS
        Error: Auth Username/Password was not provided by peer'
        hostname: 'ip-172-30-2-78'
        program_name: '(null)'
```

```
        log: 'Tue Jul  2 18:43:39 2019 192.168.0.15:58906 TLS Error:
        Auth Username/Password was not provided by peer'

**Phase 2: Completed decoding.
        decoder: 'openvpn-bad-pass'
        srcip: '192.168.0.15'

**Phase 3: Completed filtering (rules).
        Rule id: '1002'
        Level: '2'
        Description: 'Unknown problem somewhere in the system.'
**Alert to be generated.
```

You should see openvpn-bad-pass show up as the decoder in Phase
2. Great! Phase 3 rule 1002 will be what actually alerts, because
we haven't created any VPN rules yet. Paste in your HMAC line:

```
Tue Jul  2 18:45:52 2019 TLS Error: cannot locate HMAC in incoming
 packet from [AF_INET6]::ffff:192.168.0.15:39859
```

And you should see that the openvpn-bad-cert decoder matches
and also pulls the correct source IP into srcip.

Press CTRL-C to exit the decoder tool.

We could, at this point, create additional decoders to parse our
log messages to grab specific information to use later — for
example, one thing you might want to do is grab the IP from
the connection errors and use OSSEC to physically block any
further connections from that IP at the firewall. Unless you're
an OSSEC-acceptable regex master, you may find yourself
creating specific decoders for each rule type, since their format
is not necessarily consistent.

Now, we're ready to write local rules.

Crafting Custom Rules

Open /var/ossec/rules/local_rules.xml (using sudo; everything
in /var/ossec is owned by root).

First, we'll create a group, and a few "catch-all" rules to run
against any log that is decoded by our openvpn decoders.

113

We'll set the rule ID as 700000 to avoid collision; you can make this anything that won't collide with the active OSSEC ruleset (100000 or higher is safe). We set this as level 0 because we don't want it to trigger an alert:

```
<group name="local,syslog,openvpn">
<rule id="700000" level="0">
<decoded_as>openvpn-bad-pass</decoded_as>
<description>OpenVPN log entry with IP near beginning</description>
</rule>

<rule id="700010" level="0">
<decoded_as>openvpn-bad-cert</decoded_as>
<description>OpenVPN log entry with IP near end</description>
</rule>
</group>
```

Next, we add dependent rules that trigger if the action matches what's specified in the rule. <if_sid> specifies the dependency. In the following rule group, we've added two rules that alert when they see the username and password and wrong certificate errors. Notice how each of the specific rules with higher priority reference the more catch-all rules:

```
<group name="local,syslog,openvpn">
<rule id="700000" level="0">
<decoded_as>openvpn-bad-pass</decoded_as>
<description>OpenVPN log entry with IP near beginning</description>
</rule>

<rule id="700001" level="3">
  <if_sid>700000</if_sid>
  <match>TLS Error: Auth</match>
  <description>OpenVPN Bad Username or Password</description>
 <group>OpenVPN error</group>
</rule>

<rule id="700010" level="0">
<decoded_as>openvpn-bad-cert</decoded_as>
<description>OpenVPN log entry with IP near end</description>
</rule>

<rule id="700011" level="3">
  <if_sid>700010</if_sid>
  <match>TLS Error: cannot locate HMAC</match>
  <description>OpenVPN Bad Certificate</description>
 <group>OpenVPN error</group>
</rule>
</group>
```

Save your local_rules.xml file, and let's test it again, this time with a bad login message we pulled from our openvpn.log:

```
[ec2-user@~]$ sudo /var/ossec/bin/ossec-logtest
2019/07/02 21:15:25 ossec-testrule: INFO: Reading local decoder file.
2019/07/02 21:15:25 ossec-testrule: INFO: Started (pid: 21710).
ossec-testrule: Type one log per line.

Tue Jul  2 18:35:53 2019 192.168.1.15:44916 TLS Error: Auth Username/
Password was not provided by peer


**Phase 1: Completed pre-decoding.
       full event: 'Tue Jul  2 18:35:53 2019 192.168.1.15:44916 TLS
       Error: Auth Username/Password was not provided by peer'
       hostname: 'ip-172-30-2-78'
       program_name: '(null)'
       log: 'Tue Jul  2 18:35:53 2019 192.168.1.15:44916 TLS Error:
       Auth Username/Password was not provided by peer'

**Phase 2: Completed decoding.
       decoder: 'openvpn-bad-pass'
       srcip: '192.168.1.15'

**Phase 3: Completed filtering (rules).
       Rule id: '700001'
       Level: '3'
       Description: 'OpenVPN Bad Username or Password'
**Alert to be generated.
```

Now we're ready to restart OSSEC and check alerts!

```
[ec2-user@~ ]$ sudo /var/ossec/bin/ossec-control restart
```

Once you've verified that everything's working the way you want, you may want to go back into /etc/openvpn/server.conf, change log-append back to log and restart OpenVPN, since you no longer need OpenVPN to append to logs for your own testing.

Using the srcip Field to Ignore Errors from Specific Hosts

If you want to ignore alerts from specific hosts — for example, if you know that you yourself are going to disconnect and reconnect a lot in testing and don't want any alerts — you can add a rule for that inside your local rules file and within the group we created. It would look like the following (where your IP would replace 192.168.1.15:

```
<rule id="700003" level="0">
    <if_sid>700000</if_sid>
    <srcip>192.168.1.15</srcip>
    <description>Ignore errors from 192.168.1.15</description>
  </rule>
```

11

Stopping or Terminating Your AWS Instances

If you haven't exceeded your free tier usage on Amazon, you won't be charged for hours the system runs. However, if you're not using the server, there's no reason to have it continue to run (and you're still charged for any outgoing data — tiny though that may be). You have two options: You can stop the server and leave it in a suspended state to run later or terminate it to destroy it.

To stop or terminate your server on EC2:

1. Open up the Amazon Management Console and navigate to **Services > EC2 > Instances**.

2. Select the instance you want to stop, expand the **Actions** menu, and select **Instance State > Stop** or **Terminate**, depending on whether you'd like to temporarily stop or destroy the instance.

3. If you are terminating the instance and don't plan to re-assign the Elastic IP to another instance, enable the checkbox to release the Elastic IP back to Amazon before you confirm the Termination — this will prevent you from being charged for holding onto an unassigned Elastic IP.

To stop or terminate your server on Amazon Lightsail:

1. Click the ellipsis menu next to your instance listing.

2. Click **Stop** to stop or **Terminate** the instance.

12

Extending Your VPN Server

Now that you've got your secure VPN (and optionally, web) server up and running, you may find you want to enhance it. The following sections and chapters will walk through enhancements, updates, and tweaks you may want to make to improve performance and enhance security.

12.1   A Few Important Notes About Security

In this guide, we've taken some basic precautions to help secure our VPN server. In addition, we've configured AWS Security Groups to be restrictive, so that connections can only be made from our current location — but you'll find that you will want to and will need to access your VPN on-the-go. That's one of the great advantages of using a VPN — it's very easy to use with a mobile device.

You have a few options when it comes to allowing yourself access remotely: you can open your VPN port to 0.0.0.0/0 (in other words, the world) to make it easy to access from anywhere, or you can add IPs on-the-fly, wherever you are. Obviously, being restrictive is more secure and opening your VPN server up to the planet is more convenient. You should find the balance that works best for you. You can access the AWS Management Console from anywhere, even if you've locked yourself out of your own systems, from a web site or the mobile app (see *Opening Up Connections On-the-Fly with the*

Amazon AWS Console App on page 130). Thus, it's easy to let yourself back in!

If you do decide to open up your VPN server port to the world, secure it! Be sure to run some sort of monitoring system to ensure that you're alerted to any anomalous behavior or possible breaches. OSSEC is a good, light-weight option and we discussed installation and configuration in *Installing OSSEC to Monitor for Network Intrusions* on page 99. It doesn't listen on the wire, but rather monitors your web access logs in real-time to give you a heads up if anything seems awry. It also periodically runs rootkit detection and system integrity analysis.

You should consider disabling your Apache web server if you're not using it — or run it on a separate instance. It's not uncommon to double- or triple-task systems in this way, but keeping these separate will give you a smaller attack surface if your server is open to the world. And it's trivial to spin up another system for Apache — we've timed the install and configuration in this guide — after you're familiar with the process, you can launch a locked-down web server in less than five minutes!

One neat thing about AWS is that, if you *do* get breached, you can lock down access, figure out what went wrong, work out how to keep it from happening again — and launch a new instance.

With that in mind, you should use two-factor authentication on your AWS account so that no one else can access it. If you want to share duties with a coworker, friend, or family member, use reduced user roles (IAM) to do so. You can also create an IAM user whose only ability in the account is to open security groups — it might be best to set up an account like this that even you use, so that if you're trying to get in on the go, all you can do from the app is open and close ports.

12.2   Shore Up Your Key Store

OpenVPN recommends as a best practice that the system you use to generate and sign security keys and certificates (your *Certificate Authority*, or CA) be physically separate from your VPN server, and that it should reside on a secure, separate machine that is not likely not to be accessed by the outside world.

This is because, if your CA is compromised, the keys to the kingdom are lost. Or worse, they can be forged — a bad actor could use your CA to generate new, valid keys. In addition, because there's not a lot of entropy on virtual machines — which can reduce the randomness of your keys — it's a good idea to generate these keys on real hardware if you're setting up a VPN server that could be targeted by an attacker with nation-state level resources.

12.3   Require User Names and Passwords in Addition to Certificates in OpenVPN

You may want to add password protection to your clients in addition to the certificate-based authentication we're using.

1. Add the following line to your server.conf file:

```
plugin /usr/lib64/openvpn/plugins/openvpn-plugin-auth-\
pam.so login
```

2. Then add users from the shell:

```
[ec2-user~]$ sudo useradd -s /sbin/nologin vpn-user
```

3. Create a password for the user:

```
[ec2-user~]$ sudo passwd vpn-user
```

4. Restart OpenVPN:

```
[ec2-user~]$ sudo systemctl stop openvpn
[ec2-user~]$ sudo systemctl start openvpn
```

5. Regenerate your client configuration files:

```
[ec2-user~]$ cd ~/diy-vpn/mkcliconf && sudo \
python mkcliconf.py
```

6. Copy your new configuration files to your secure site, and download and install them on the devices you want to use:

```
[ec2-user~]$ sudo cp server_name.* /var/www/html/downloads && \
sudo chown apache:apache /var/www/html/downloads/
```

12.4 Assigning a Domain Name Using Amazon Route 53

Should you decide that you want to use your secure web site in a more permanent way, it's a good idea to give your site a domain name. It's also a lot easier to remember or share and, using AWS tools, you can swap out the underlying server whenever you want, keeping your IP address and domain the same.

In this section, we'll talk about registering a new domain, connecting it to your server using Amazon Web Services, and obtaining and installing CA-issued SSL certificates to ensure traffic to and from the Apache web server is secured. If you already own the domain name you'd like to use, there are a number of configurations you can use, but for the purposes of our guide, we'll assume you're starting from scratch.

Registering a Domain Name with Route 53

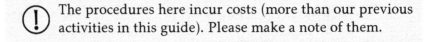 The procedures here incur costs (more than our previous activities in this guide). Please make a note of them.

1. Open the Amazon Web Services Management Console and tap **Services** > **Network and Content Delivery** > **Route 53**. The Route 53 page opens.

2. Type the domain name you'd like to check for in the **Register Domain** list and click **Check.** If you're lucky, your domain will be available. If not, keep trying!

3. Click **Add to Cart** next to any domain you'd like to purchase, then click **Continue.**

4. When prompted, enter **Registrant Contact** information (this is either your information or your company's) and click **Continue.**

   You should use the Hide option, if available. Disreputable companies harvest whois information from domain registrars, and that's just one more way to try to protect yourself. If someone needs to contact you about the domain, they'll go through your registrar (in this case, Amazon) and you'll get the message. Note that some types of domain names do not allow you to hide your personal information, such as .us, .ca, .cn.

5. The Review and Purchase page appears. Read and accept the terms, then click **Continue.**

Now, we wait. If this is the first domain you've registered with Amazon, be sure to periodically check your email for a verification request, which is typically sent within a few minutes. While Amazon states that it may take up to three days for Amazon to confirm and register your domain, in most cases, it takes just a few minutes.

You can check status at any time by going to **Route 53 > Domains > Pending Requests.**

Associating Your New Domain with Your Server

After Amazon has approved your domain registration, you're ready to associate your new domain name with your server. We'll create two new "A" type records to associate www.domain_name.com and domain_name.com with our server.

Note that Amazon currently charges $.50 per month per hosted zone for up to month for your first 25 hosted zones (additional hosted zones over 25 are $.10/month). As with all things Amazon, these prices are correct at time of writing but are subject to change — be sure to double-check!

To associate your new domain with your web server:

1. From the AWS Management Console, navigate to **Services > Network and Content Delivery > Route 53**.

2. Click **Hosted Zones**. The list of hosted zones will appear.

3. Select the zone that corresponds to the domain name you purchased or transferred to Amazon. Hosted Zone Details appear on the right side of the page.

> *(i)* If you're using your own domain at a separate registrar, you should create a new hosted zone for your domain here. Refer to Amazon's documentation about hosted zones at http://docs.aws.amazon.com/Route53/latest/ DeveloperGuide/CreatingHostedZone.html for more information.

4. Click **Go to Record Sets** at the top of the page. The record sets for your host zone appear.

5. Click **Create Record Set**. Record Set options appear on the right side of the page.

6. In the **Name** field, enter www.

7. In the **Type** field, select **A — IPv4 address**.

8. In the **Value** field, enter the IP of your host (a static, Elastic IP, is recommended here).

9. Click **Create**.

10. Click **Create a Record Set** to create an additional set.

11. Leave the **Name** field blank.

12. In the **Type** field, select **A — IPv4 address.**

13. In the **Value** field, enter the IP of your host (a static, Elastic IP, is recommended here).

14. Click **Create.**

Your record is created! After a few minutes, you should be able to visit https://www.your_domain.com/ to access your site. Note that propagation may take up to 30 minutes. (And technically can take days to propagate throughout the Internet and has been known to take hours...don't ask me how I know this...however, I have never, on Amazon in the last several years, had DNS propagation for my new domains take longer than 30 minutes to get to the majors. But your mileage, as always, may vary!)

You may notice an issue now, however, when you access your site: your security certificate is no longer valid! But that's great, actually — because now you can install a *real* TLS certificate! If you're purchasing a certificate from a Certificate Authority, follow your CA's instructions. Or, jump to the next section to install an SSL certificate using LetsEncrypt.

You'll also need to modify /etc/httpd/conf/httpd.conf to use your server name instead of IP in the ServerName and VirtualHost directives.

Installing an SSL Certificate with LetsEncrypt

If you want a secure site without spending a lot of money with registrars, LetsEncrypt is a great alternative. Their certificates are accepted by most browsers and authorities. The only drawback is that you've got to renew them every three months, but this is easily overcome by running a periodic script via the system scheduler (cron) to update your certificates automatically.

1. After assigning your host a domain name and verifying you can access it, log into your server and comment out the redirect that we created back when we installed our Apache server to force http to https, then restart the web server:

```
sudo sed -i 's/Redirect \/ https/#Redirect \/ https/g' \
/etc/httpd/conf/httpd.conf

[ec2-user~]$ sudo systemctl restart httpd
```

We're doing this so that LetsEncrypt will be able to access your server and won't be redirected to our https site with the self-signed certificate. Also, if you have not yet opened ports 80 and 443 up to the world using EC2 from the AWS Management Console, now is the time to do it! LetsEncrypt will need to be able to connect to your web server in order to issue an SSL certificate.

2. Install certbot and its dependencies:

```
[ec2-user~]$ sudo yum -y install certbot
```

3. Run certbot in certonly mode:

```
[ec2-user~]$ sudo certbot certonly
```

4. When prompted to select an installation type, type 2 to place files in a webroot directory, since we already have a web server running.

5. When prompted, enter the email address you want EFF to use for renewal reminders and security alerts and press Enter.

6. Read the Terms of Service and type **A** if you agree to proceed.

7. Type **Y** to allow EFF to email you about EFF news, or **N** to disallow.

8. When prompted, enter the domain names you want to protect, separated by commas or spaces. Typically, you'll do both the bare and www sites, for example, `www.mydomain.com mydomain.com`.

9. Certbot will perform some challenges and will then ask you to enter your webroot. For our installation, this is `/var/www/html`. You'll be prompted for both the bare and www site — when prompted the second time, choose 2 to select the same web root.

10. Certbot will copy your certificates to `/etc/letsencrypt/live/` *domain.com/*.

11. Open the file `/etc/httpd/conf.d/ssl.conf` and replace the following lines:

```
SSLCertificateFile /etc/pki/tls/certs/localhost.crt
SSLCertificateKeyFile /etc/pki/tls/private/localhost.key
#SSLCertificateChainFile /etc/pki/tls/certs/server-chain.crt
```

with:

```
SSLCertificateFile /etc/letsencrypt/live/mydomain.com/cert.pem
SSLCertificateKeyFile /etc/letsencrypt/live/mydomain.com/privkey.pem
SSLCertificateChainFile /etc/letsencrypt/live/mydomain.com/fullchain.pem
```

Note that LetsEncrypt now supports wildcard certificates, which means that if you ask for www.my_domain.com and domain.com, they provide you with a single certificate that works for both.

Open your web site with https:// in a browser — it should be secure now! You may also want to go back into you `httpd.conf` and uncomment the Redirect you commented out at the beginning of the procedure so that all accesses happen using https again (be sure to restart httpd after the change!).

As we discussed previously, LetsEncrypt certificates expire after three months — but we can automate certificate renewal, see the next section for instructions.

Configuring Periodic LetsEncrypt Certificate Renewals

We can configure a cron job on our server to automatically renew our LetsEncrypt SSL certificates.

1. Log into your server and open /etc/cron.d/crontab:

   ```
   [ec2-user~]$ sudo nano /etc/cron.d/crontab
   ```

2. Add the following line:

```
0  1,13 *  *  *    root  /usr/bin/certbot renew --no-self-upgrade
```

What does this do? This adds the certbot renew task to the system scheduler. The first five parts, typically delineated by asterisks, stand for the minute, hour, day, week, and month, followed by the user who should run the command, and the command itself. You can separate the values by one or more spaces; they are ignored by the the system.

In this example, we see that the root user will run the certbot renew process (and will not automatically update the client), every day at 1:00AM and 1:00PM (system time, UTC, so exact time may differ based on *your* time zone).

12.5 Using iptables to Block Access to Your Systems

If you're using Lightsail, you may notice one limitation — the Amazon UI doesn't allow you to block public access to any port you open. This can open you up to brute force attacks from hackers and bots trying to log in. Because you have some control of the system, you can use its own firewall to block access. The port we'll want to close to the world is 22 — we use this port to SSH into our system, but we don't serve anything publicly, and because, on Lightsail, you can always access the console from the web site, it's less important that we can access it from a mobile connection.

So let's use the following procedure to update iptables' INPUT chain, which controls incoming packets, to block incoming network access to port 22 to anyone but ourselves.

1. Open the Lightsail console, tap the menu next to your instance, and select **Connect**.

2. Type last to show the last IP addresses that accessed the system; this will show our internal network via the web console. For instance, if all connections came from between 72.21.217.1 through 72.21.217.255, we can assume Amazon is using this network block to manage Lightsail.

3. Once in, enter the following command to allow the web-based console connection (72.21.217.0/8), the internal EC2 network (172.0.0.0/12), the internal VPN network (10.0.0.0/8), the VPN server's external address (s.s.s.s/32 below; add your VPN server's external IP here instead) and any IP address you normally use to connect via SSH into the system:

```
sudo iptables -A INPUT -p tcp -s 172.0.0.0/12 --dport 22 -j ACCEPT
sudo iptables -A INPUT -p tcp -s 10.0.0.0/8 --dport 22 -j ACCEPT
sudo iptables -A INPUT -p tcp -s 72.21.217.0/24 --dport 22 -j ACCEPT
sudo iptables -A INPUT -p tcp -s s.s.s.s/32 --dport 22 -j ACCEPT
sudo iptables -A INPUT -p tcp -s y.y.y.y/32 --dport 22 -j ACCEPT
```

4. Run the following command to show your changes to the INPUT chain and review them. Make sure they are correct or you may be locked out (restart the system to clear the rules if you goof up!):

```
[ec2-user~]$ sudo iptables -L INPUT
```

5. If you need to delete any rules, use the same syntax, but replace the -A with a -D, for example:

```
sudo iptables -D INPUT -p tcp -s 172.0.0.0/12 --dport 22 -j ACCEPT
```

6. Once you've got these in, you're ready to block port 22 to everyone else:

```
[ec2-user~]$ sudo iptables -A INPUT -p tcp --dport 22 -j DROP
```

7. Make sure you still have access! If not, you can reboot the system to clear your changes. If the changes are good and you can still access your server via SSH, save your changes and restart:

```
sudo service iptables save && sudo service
iptables restart
```

If you're logged on using the web console, you may get kicked off during restart. You can click Reconnect to reconnect.

And that's it! No more brute force attacks on your SSH port and, if you're using OSSEC and have seen alerts for those attacks, you should stop seeing them.

12.6 Opening Up Connections On-the-Fly with the Amazon AWS Console App

Should you decide to keep your VPN server selectively locked down, the Amazon Console mobile app adds some convenience in that it allows you to update your AWS security group wherever you are and is available via the Amazon Appstore, Apple App Store, and Google Play.

12.7 Adding IPv6 Support to Your VPN

In our example, we use an AWS instance that, by default, does not support IPv6. What we did to avoid IPv6 requests from IPv6-enabled devices "leaking" outside the VPN was to push routes down to the clients that told them to route all IPv6 traffic through the VPN. Amazon *does* have IPv6-enabled instances and OpenVPN version 2.4 supports IPv6 forwarding. Amazon's IPv6-enabled instances require you to create a new VPC (or virtual private cloud) that is IPv6-enabled. As most sites haven't cut off IPv4 users yet, IPv6 is a nice-to-have, but not a requirement for a private home VPN right now — but it's something you may want to consider!

13

Further Reading

There's a wealth of great information at our fingertips! Check out the following for additional information you can use to expand your deployment. Email vpn@diy-vpn.com with any questions, comments, or errata:

The OpenVPN 2.4 Manual:

https://community.openvpn.net/openvpn/wiki/Openvpn24ManPage

Hardening OpenVPN:

https://community.openvpn.net/openvpn/wiki/Hardening

Apache 2.4 documentation:

https://httpd.apache.org/docs/2.4/

Apache Security Tips:

https://httpd.apache.org/docs/2.4/misc/ security_tips.html

OSSEC documentation:

https://ossec.github.io/docs/

Securing EC2 Instances:

https://aws.amazon.com/blogs/security/how-to-protect-data-at-rest-with-amazon-ec2-instance-store-encryption/

Bibliography

[1] Katie Hafner. Seeing Corporate Fingerprints in Wikipedia Edits. https://www.nytimes.com/2007/08/19/technology/19wikipedia.html.

[2] Tom Brant. Netflix Aims to Shield Your TV Habits from Prying Eyes. https://www.pcmag.com/news/347132/netflix-aims-to-shield-your-tv-habits-from-prying-eyes.

[3] David Kravets. Comcast Wi-Fi serving self-promotional ads via Javascript injection, 2014. https://arstechnica.com/tech-policy/2014/09/why-comcasts-javascript-ad-injections-threaten-security-net-neutrality/.

[4] Muhammad Ikram, Narseo Vallina-Rodriguez, Suranga Seneviratne, Mohamed Ali Ikram, Narseo Vallina-Rodriguez, Suranga Seneviratne, Mohamed Ali Kaafar, and Vern Paxson. An analysis of the Privacy and Security Risks of Android VPN Permission-enabled Apps. https://research.csiro.au/ng/wp-content/uploads/sites/106/2016/08/paper-1.pdf.